EMOTIONALLY CHARGED LEARNING

SECRETS TO COMPETITIVE ADVANTAGES FOR THE SECOND HALF OF THE KNOWLEDGE/ENTERTAINMENT-BASED ECONOMY

ERIC SCHIFFER

Literary Press

Emotionally Charged Learning
Copyright 2003 Eric Schiffer. All rights reserved.

ISBN No. 0-9716958--2-2
Library of Congress Control No. 2002113484

Dedication

To Suzzy
For your inspiration

CONTENTS

Foreword vii
Introduction ix

Part I
What in the world is going on? The Current Realities You Face 1
What is Emotionally Charged Learning? 12

Part II
The Science of: EMOTIONS, MEMORY and LEARNING 17
Applying Modern Marketing Techniques to
    Entertainment and Learning 55
The Entertainment Economy 62
    The Role of Music in Learning 74
    The Role of Television and Movies in Learning 80

Part III
The Business of Learning 87
The Case for E-Learning 87
Retention and Performance-Transfer 95
Profitability and ROI 99

Part IV
How Can Your Company Benefit from Emotionally
    Charged Learning 115

FOREWORD
Bob Nelson, Ph.D.

If you're like most people you've sat through tens of thousands of boring learning experiences in classrooms throughout your entire life. Rarely did you feel engaged and excited about the process or topics discussed. Seldom still did you retain much of anything that you heard. Yet, in short order you accepted this ineffective process as the norm and it connoted "learning" to you in your life.

It's easy with such a common experience for us all to become jaded as to the limitations of the process of education. Instead of demanding something better, we tended to lower our expectations and abandon all hopes that the process could be different, not to even consider improved. We became complacent about one of the most basic and important of life skills: learning.

Yet somehow we muddled through and proceeded in one way or another to inflict the same pain and approach to those that followed, be they our children or our employees. As adults this negative experience carried into our jobs and became perpetuated through training experiences that did little to improve the dynamics of learning at work.

In this fast-moving and captivating book, Eric Schiffer makes the case for why our past experience with education, its flaws and limitations, need not limit our present experience. He shows how the discipline of training is actively being redefined to better meet the needs and demands of a new, different work force that has new and different aptitudes. He lays the foundation for how the best learning today engages people in an intentional way that in the past may only have happened on occasion by accident.

In this book, Eric defines a new vision for learning he calls Emotionally Charged Learning (ECL). In it he describes how an integration of the senses needs to occur to maximize the retention of anything we hope to truly learn and retain for our long-term benefit—a process in which learning needs to take place at all levels and how the spirit as well as the intellect needs to be engaged. He shows how our emotions can be harnessed and aligned with the systematic adaptation of the right combination of techniques and that in so doing, a magical process opens up to us that allows us to learn in both a more efficient and fun manner. He explains how the mind works to capture and integrate those life experiences that are most necessary for our survival. With ECL the possibilities that we might only have imagined in the past can happen today.

Well researched and documented, this book makes the case for how the forces of education and entertainment have merged with a vengeance to make learning today both a dynamic and exciting process well within the reach of every trainer, educator, manager and employee. He further makes the case for why this new approach to learning is not only possible, but also essential for both employers and employees alike.

This book describes the important link between learning and emotion and how to intentionally intertwine the two to create new levels of retention. It shows how the best learning is, in fact, fun as well and describes why the power of storytelling works and how music has been shown to impact learning. These connections are not coincidences but rather direct links between our emotional experiences and the applied results.

Prepare to open your mind to some possibilities that seem both new and yet somehow familiar at the same time. This book will help you integrate what you know with what you feel. It will help you merge understanding with experience—and enjoy doing so in a way you've never imagined possible.

Bob Nelson, Ph.D.
President, Nelson Motivation Inc. and
Author of *1001 Ways to Reward Employees*

INTRODUCTION

Einstein said, "All of the information that ever has been, or ever will be is already here. Our challenge is to find it."

Not so long ago, we lived in an industrial economy. More recently it has been referred to as the "information age." In reality, we live in a "knowledge" based economy, not just an information age.

To paraphrase Einstein, Information is everywhere. What is at a premium is knowledge—what we *do* with what we *discover*. In other words, if we don't learn from the information we find, purchase or are given, it is useless because to fully use the information, we must first learn something from it that we did not previously know, and then add value to it by giving it purpose, by putting it to use. That use could be anything from enhancing a personal relationship, to serving our customers better, to changing the world as we know it. This book is about all those things and more. You will discover the importance that emotion plays in all kinds of learning and how you can apply this knowledge to get results in your business immediately.

Learning, by its very nature, can be an extremely passionate experience, indeed it must be. I have studied the science and art of learning, and more particularly the role that emotion plays in the process, most of my adult life. I know from those academic and practical experiences that "real" learning can not take place without emotion. There can be no discovery, no innovation, no value created or added if we are not passionately involved in the material and the process of learning. If information and its delivery, i.e., teaching or facilitating, is not emotionally charged, it is not retained, and if it is not retained, it can't be used. It simply remains "information," which is little more than type on a page, zeros and ones passing through computer chips, or sound and light waves meandering through space.

What is ECL?

It is an edge-of-your-seat learning experience that leaves an emotional imprint on your total being: mind, body and spirit. It is an adventure that stirs your imagination and charges your own creativity. The memory of it drives you to thirst for more of the same in all your subsequent experiences. *ECL is ultimately at the core of what you are capable of becoming.* That is why, after you have experienced it, you will forever thereafter compare each new bit of information, each teacher, book, seminar, classroom, newspaper article or TV news broadcast you encounter with your ECL experience. And you will ask, "Why can't all learning be this powerful and entertaining, this compelling, this useful, this much fun?" The answer, is, it can if it's emotionally charged.

In that context, think about what the face of science, art or medicine would look like today if Einstein had not had a passion for quantum physics. What if Michaelangelo had not had an unquenchable thirst for understanding the human anatomy? Imagine if Jonas Salk had not had an abiding love and concern for the well-being of his fellow man.

> Enjoy!
> Eric Schiffer
> Chairman and CEO
> Trainingscape, Inc.

PART ONE

TODAY . . .

Technology is not compassionate, sympathetic or gentle. It crashes into existing systems with a take-no-prisoners approach while it simultaneously destroys them, creating new ones in its wake. You can get crushed trying to stop it, or you can surf the powerful waves of change to wonderful new worlds. Companies, indeed entire nations, and those who lead them have choices.

Those who ride the crest will move at warp speed just to keep up. This is the knowledge/entertainment-based economy: a world charged with emotion as well as intellect, the most competitive environment humankind has ever known, a highly sophisticated economy that literally changes day by day.

How will you and your company approach it? How will you not only keep up, but exceed beyond your current dreams? In a moment, we will discuss what the current realities of the second half of the knowledge/entertainment economy portend for your business.

Today's business stars are KNOWLEDGE MASTERS! We have gone from muscles to neurons in the blink of an eye. Our business processes are built upon it.

Simply put, the value of your organization is directly related to the amount of knowledge that your people gain, retain and best utilize.

If you question this for even a second, imagine all of your top people coming into work tomorrow with amnesia that won't go away.

EMOTIONALLY CHARGED LEARNING

WHAT IN THE WORLD IS GOING ON?
The Current Realities That You Face

TWO THIRDS OF THE WORLD'S ECONOMY IS *KNOWLEDGE-BASED,* and growing daily.

ARE YOUR EMPLOYEES KNOWLEDGE MASTERS? Will your company ride the powerful waves of change to a wonderful new world, or will your business be swept away by the Tsunami of your competition's intelligence and the speeding bullet of technology? Let's take a moment to look at what is going on in the knowledge-based world.

If you are in business today you recognize that the world is moving away from making things you can feel and touch to more intangible elements such as technology, science and "service." In the knowledge economy, one of your biggest investments is in attracting and keeping smart people and helping them to become even smarter.

Since most value created within the service economy is knowledge-based, those with the knowledge are the ones getting richer. As a product becomes standardized and is mass-produced, whether it's a gadget, a seed or a software program, the KNOWLEDGE COMPONENET BECOMES MORE IMPORTANT than the manual labor it takes to produce it. I love this example: In 1984 when cell phones were introduced, they cost approximately $4,000 apiece. Today they are FREE (with activation). Why? Because it costs practically nothing to make them, but more importantly, manufacturers eventually wised up and realized the profits were not in the sale of the product, they were made on the airtime. Now, even the once very lucrative business of selling airtime is in jeopardy. Not long ago, in fact just a couple of years ago, long distance telephone calls were an expensive service. Today, huge companies like AT+T and others are going nuts trying to figure out how they're going to make money when everyone is using the Internet and wireless phones, beaming their calls across cyberspace instead of copper wires.

PART ONE

Knowledgable people produce more ... and make FEWER MISTAKES!

All of this is why one of your responsibilities as a leader is to insure that this generation (of your employees), as well as the next, is more knowledgeable.

In the knowledge-based economy, the companies that grow the fastest are those selling ideas, not necessarily those with the most physical assets. As an example, General Motors was incorporated in 1916 and today it sells in fifty-two countries. On the other hand, Microsoft was only founded in 1975 and it sells in sixty-three countries and growing.

Because of being a knowledge-based economy where information and learning are our assets, the world now is nearly without economic borders and ...

... with interactive multimedia systems, management in developing countries can bypass the industrial revolution altogether—and they are!

We are in the middle of history's newest and most powerful revolution. It took 500 million years to go from the first "brains," i.e., simple nervous systems, to the invention of television (1926). It took less than 60 years to go from there to wireless computers, fiber optics and a world economy almost entirely dependent upon knowledge and instantaneous communication (muscle power to neuron skills).

The new catalysts are the convergence of computer technology, television, entertainment and instant communication (Internet, wireless devices). These converging technologies have tremendous implications for education with the potential to bypass traditional teaching and learning, i.e., public schools, as surely as developing nations are hop-scotching the industrial revolution.

In the 1950s, 65 percent of the American workforce was blue-collar. Now it's only 13 percent and falling. That doesn't mean we are producing less (approximately 24 percent of America's GNP is in manufacturing, about the same as it has been for 40 years or so).

Obviously, that 24 percent of GNP represents many more products now than then. So, what is the big change other than the fact that the the economy has grown tremendously overall?

The big difference is that WE ARE NOW MANUFACTURING WITH INFORMATION, WITH COMPUTERS AND AUTOMATION INSTEAD OF PEOPLE.

That 13 percent workforce will continue to shrink, just as the agricultural base has gone from a time when 90 percent of the population were farmers, two-hundred years ago, to today where they represent less than 3 percent of the population.

John Naisbitt, co-author of, **Megatrands** and **Reinventing The Corporation,** predicts that early in the 21st century, only ten percent of the workforce in affluent nations will be working in direct manufacturing. The question then becomes, if all of a country's manufacturing can be done by 10 percent of its population, what are the other 90 percent of the citizens going to do?

Obviously, every person and every company has to become the manager of his, her, or its own future. However, a great deal of our education still looks like the declining industrial methods of manufacturing. From grade school through college and then into the workplace on an on-going manner, educational systems resemble the standard assembly line (not much different than Henry Ford's first plant), with curriculum divided into subjects, taught in units, arranged by grade, and controlled by standardized tests. (Please bear with me while I take a short power nap). .

PART ONE

This system is no longer representative of the world in which we live! Traditional learning methods can no longer cope with the realities of a knowledge-based economy.

Information-based economies need fewer people. Consider that many of McDonald's 23,000 franchises around the world are run by husband-and-wife teams, all linked to one central system. Further, consider that 20 million Americans are now making money from home-based industries and over 60 percent of them are women.

The smallest companies are vital and it's the young entrepreneurial companies that create most of the new jobs in the U.S. In the 1980s, America created 22 million brand-new jobs and 90 percent of those 22 million were companies with less than 50 employees. This sector is still what is creating the wealth. In many of these companies, the educational need is for THINKING and CONCEPTUAL skills, risk-taking and experimentation. How much of that is taught in schools or through traditional curriculums?

If you are the CEO, CLO, or the head of Human Resources of a large company, take heart. General Electric with thousands of employees is still one of the premier organizations in the world and it looks as if it will maintain its standing for some time to come. My illustrations about "fewer and smaller" are mostly to drive home my point about the importance of knowledge. However, I agree with R. Buckminster Fuller, the renowned architect and brilliant thinker who postulated many years ago that the universe, and by extension, humankind's endeavors, were constantly expanding and contracting—simultaneously. While the big bang theory would suggest that all of matter is expanding, i.e., shooting further and further into deeper and deeper space, it is also contracting, or trying to pull back to its center. It is this magnificent balance of tension that makes life possible. Likewise, our own universe on earth is expanding and contracting in much the same manner. Though our economy is larger than ever before, our GNP remains nearly static, even shrinking slightly. Where once it took 100 workers to make a widget, it now takes no workers, just a few robotic arms directed and managed by a software program running on an unmanned computer.

Nano technology is now de rigueur. According to Juan Enriquez in his book, *As the Future Catches You*,

"We can already produce very small things. Japanese engineers have produced a car that looks and operates like any other with one glaring exception: it is the size of a grain of rice!" He continues, *"The first computer chips were marvels. They integrated hundreds of circuits on a small piece of silicon. However, building faster, more powerful computers required packing more and more components in increasingly smaller and smaller spaces. We have gotten very good at this. Some chips built this year (2002) contain close to a billion components.*

"When manufacturers polish the surface of chips today, the error tolerance is 0.15 microns (a micron is a millionth of a meter), or about one ten-thousandths of the width of one of your hairs.

"But shortly, even these manufacturing standards will seem crude because various companies and labs are now experimenting with products built on a nano scale. When you build things on a nano scale, they are measured in BILLIONTHS of a meter. You could literally write your name using individual atoms (this is already a reality). To put this in perspective, you could write the entire Encyclopedia Britannica *on the head of a pin!"*

My own research lab in the area of nanotech is working on some very interesting discoveries in the area of training, as well.

Only you know exactly how your company uses knowledge, or can imagine how it will use it in the future. That is proprietary to your business, whether that's manufacturing or service-based.

One very successful company, The Container Store, believes that their "people" are at least as vital to increasing sales or keeping up with their inventory. Each employee is obligated to 235 hours of product training in their first year and 162 hours each year thereafter. A staggering amount considering the industry average is just 10 hours a year!

As you might guess, The Container Store is quite adept at retaining their good "people," (which of course is another serendipitous fallout of teaching and training your employees, in addition to increased productivity and revenue). 94 percent of the employees of The Container Store that were randomly surveyed said that "respect" played a huge role in their decision to continue working there. They felt they made a difference.

These employees no doubt felt that the fact that the company was willing to spend that much time and money educating them was a definitive statement about their worth as people, not just employees (and I'm sure their customers sense this).

Obviously, The Container Store understands the value of employee development:

SMARTER EMPLOYEES, ENHANCED LOYALTY, LESS TURN OVER, HAPPIER CUSTOMERS, INCREASED REVENUE, are but just a few of the benefits of having smarter employees.

IT'S ALL SIMPLY ECONOMIC DARWINISM.

Smarter employees means your company . . .

is more competitive . . .
is more efficient . . .
has fewer problems (perhaps fewer lawsuits i.e., sexual harassment, managing workplace violence, etc., etc.) . . .
can be more profitable . . .
is quicker to market . . ..
etc., etc., etc.

In today's information-based economy people can not only communicate instantly around and into almost every nook and cranny of the globe, they can train and LEARN INSTANTLY.

> *"EVERY COMPANY WILL BECOME AN*
> *EDUCATION COMPANY OR IT WILL FAIL."*
> — Don Tappscott,
> **Blueprint To The Digital Economy**

In short, this means the survival of the smartest. Your strongest competitors are getting smarter every day, in every way. They are doing things better, faster, cheaper. Like countries, companies that educate their own are the ones that are getting richer. The key question then becomes, "How do we choose to educate our own?" What techniques do we use to insure that our employees are GETTING IT, and KEEPING IT, and in turn, USING IT?

How can an organization stand out from the competition when everyone has access to the same technology, markets and sources of capital? Simply put . . . **with its people.** In economic Darwinism, not only the smartest survive, but to use Charles Darwin's own words, "It's not the strongest of the species who survive, nor the most intelligent, but the ones most responsive to change." Emotionally Charged Learning is change—decidedly for the better.

Every manager, executive and employee must master a broader range of skills to continue to compete. With more to learn and less time to learn it, what can organizations do to keep up? If your company wants to improve speed to market, enhance customer service levels, improve productivity, create employee innovation and enhance retention levels, then you must embrace the new SCIENCE and ART of EMOTIONALLY CHARGED LEARNING through a blended process combining online (e-learning) and live training.

In today's knowledge-based economy, we are no longer about physical assets. Our assets are brain cells, synapses, dendrites and EMOTIONAL INTELLIGENCE. The reality is that human knowledge (like the convergence of computer technology, nano-research, proteomics, bioinformatics and genomics) changes, moves faster and is more efficient and creative by the hour, day and week—not years. In this world, the lack of quality human assets in your business will translate to great pain, loss of revenue, productivity and/or clients, and eventually your demise (technology is not compassionate, sympathetic or gentle). Without a doubt, human capital is the cornerstone of this economy and it is central to the value of your company and your ability to innovate—now and in the future.

One of the future's biggest global competitors understands this. Today, China has a national mandate to educate their people by spending 25 percent of every company's budget on education and training. In Taiwan, a national mandate from 1996 has come true as every single school in the country now has a computer for every two children. Most children have their own web sites by age 10.

Over 50 percent of any given company's expenses lies in payroll. Yet, with all the focus on process improvement over the last twenty years, the largest single expense on the payroll has never been "reengineered" for maximum efficiency on a consistent organization-by-organization basis. Why? Because we have looked at enhancing human capital as a COST, not an INVESTMENT. We must begin today, this moment, to enhance human capital to gain significant competitive advantages by incorporating the best practices and skills in all our people.

THE BEST COMPANIES AND TOP BUSINESS LEADERS UNDERSTAND THIS.

They realize that they have to infuse new skills into their people to compete not only with the company next door, or in another state, but across the globe.

Today's leading CEOs, CLOs and HR directors know that the biggest challenges to date have been the various ways to achieve this in the most cost-effective and result-producing way that keeps people ENGAGED, but also ensures that the LEARNING STICKS! Like any good investment, learning must transfer in very tangible ways to the workplace. We can no more afford to invest in training that is not RETAINED and UTILIZED to its maximum, than we can afford to continue to pour billions of dollars into technology that is obsolete next month. And that is just what is happening. The ugly truth is . . .

. . . most training doesn't work!

Even creative new e-learning models that might at first seem innovative, have fallen woefully short in transferring enhanced competencies to the workplace in tangible ways that vividly demonstrate high returns on investments.

Companies that have invested millions in training or e-learning, are not renewing agreements because their user rates are extremely low and their people don't like it because they are not engaged by it. No engagement means no learning.

And as you are probably already painfully aware, it isn't easy to consistently engage employees in the learning process, especially when it involves a cost-effective company-wide solution. Problems abound from ever-increasing job complexity, constantly changing business processes, short product life cycles, geographic dispersion and employee mobility—all challenging even the best organizations.

Another very real problem is that our people live in the greatest entertainment environment ever known. Today, trainers and e-learning programs must compete in a high-energy, entertainment-driven culture, i.e., movies, music videos, video games, live sporting events and other forms of entertainment. (There are more than 430,000 registered players worldwide who play a single computer game called *EverQuest*, a sort of computer-driven *Dungeons and Dragons*—and that's just one game).

People are conditioned to this level of engagement. If they don't get it, they tune out. No attention—no learning. And even attention is not enough by itself. What is learned must be RETAINED and put to IMMEDIATE USE.

What do a majority of people do with their discretionary time and money? A great deal of their time is spent going to movies and watching television. And when it is time for them to be trained, the old ways of doing it (out-dated training techniques), just don't get it done anymore. They cannot begin to compete for ATTENTION.

We all know that effective learning is what sets the great companies apart from the merely good ones. GE was a leader for years under Jack Welch because of his relentless focus on infusing his leadership team and employees with the most effective expertise and knowledge possible. He did a lot of it with his senior leaders and himself. He used conflict. He challenged them. It was pure entertainment and they learned.

Since our people are our most important assets, we must also remember we are all emotional animals. We want to be stimulated and engaged in everything we do, from our leisure time to the time we spend at the grocery store. Is it entertainment or is it business? The fact is, the line has forever been crossed and blurred. The relationship is symbiotic, each filling a need for the other. When a teenage girl buys a pair of jeans at the department store because the sound track from Titanic is playing over the loud speaker, is that clothes shopping or a lust for Leonardo? You will see later in this book why you're not only competing with other companies in a knowledge-based economy, you're competing against the entertainment industry. There are companies like Universal Studios with $6 billion in annual earnings, Blockbuster Video does $4 billion annually, Playboy Enterprises earns $300 million, the music industry in general is now a $14 billion industry, and I would argue that Hugh Hefner is a more recognizable name than John Reed (co-chairman of Citigroup).

These types of companies have conditioned your people to want experiences they will remember. If you give them what they need to learn during an Emotionally Charged experience, it will stick and they will learn. We need to harness what people are already conditioned to doing. To do less than this is not productive. People are conditioned to entertainment that packs an emotional punch.

Michael Porter's work on competitive business advantages highlights the fact that we must maintain a UNIQUE DIFFERENCE that cannot be achieved by our competition. How do your people help you achieve this difference? When you answer that, ask yourself: What are the knowledge components that make that possible? What are the skills and competencies that are the backbone of that knowledge? How can you transfer those skills through your organization, keep your people fully engaged emotionally and then insure they retain what they've learned—and further guarantee that the new knowledge is implemented immediately and effectively?

How will you compete in this knowledge/entertainment-based economy for the emotions and minds of your people?

Can you begin to more clearly see the benefits of Emotionally Charged Learning? When do you think will be the best time for you and your organization to start thinking about it?

WHAT IS EMOTIONALLY CHARGED LEARNING?

e-mo-tion *n.* 1. a) strong feeling; excitement. b) a state of consciousness having to do with the arousal of feelings, distinguished from other mental states as cognition, volition, and awareness of physical sensation.

charged *v.* 1. a) to saturate. b). to load or fill to capacity. c). to add an electrical charge.

learn-ing *n.* 1. The acquiring of knowledge or skill.

Can learning actually be "emotionally charged," to the point of a constant "arousal" of feelings, or a physical sensation? Of course it can. In fact, I propose that:

> IT IS THE ONLY WAY THAT WE CAN LEARN AND RETAIN INFORMATION IN A MEANINGFUL WAY.

You will see why as you get a little further on in this book. The secrets to competitive advantages in a knowledge/entertainment-based economy quite simply lie in Emotionally Charged Learning. It is the way that you and your people will achieve a UNIQUE DIFFERENCE. It is the wisest, most practical and tangible investment that you can make in your most important assets—your people. But, before I talk about applying ECL to your business to achieve competitive advantages, you have to know more about what it is, and why it is so superior to any other form or training used today.

Have you ever listened to a motivational speaker or attended a training session where you were so charged up, you felt utterly empowered, and couldn't wait to put what you learned to work?

Were you ever enthralled with a college professor's ability to both entertain and teach you? Did you look forward to his or her class more than any other?

Did you ever learn something that was so exciting, you set the alarm extra early so you would get to work before anyone else and experiment with the new knowledge?

EMOTIONALLY CHARGED LEARNING

Have you ever learned something new and compelling from a movie or a book, so much so that it was almost like an epiphany?

I have.

I have been fortunate enough to experience these kinds of exhilarating learning situations and many more. Of course, I've also had my share of dull and meaningless classes, seminars and speakers, as I know you have.

What did these dramatic experiences have in common for me? Unlike my boring encounters, I was fully engaged: heart, mind, body and soul. Every part of me was connected and I was entertained, so much so, I never forgot those moments or most of the content.

For a moment close your eyes and try to remember the last time you saw a good movie, one that kept you on the edge of your seat, perhaps made you cry or laugh, or both. You probably remember it quite clearly because you were thoroughly entertained. Being entertained, you also RETAINED the memory of it. Because you were emotionally engaged in the characters and the story, you GOT IT. You walked away from the theatre with an experience (you probably learned something as well), that will remain with you for many, many years. Nearly the same thing applies to reading a great book, though in a book, your own imagination is brought into play more than in a movie.

What makes a movie or book entertaining? It could be the grand scenes that you see, or are described to you. It could be the intricate and compelling story or plot, and certainly, it is partly that. However, for the most part, it is the emotion that you feel vicariously through the characters and how they experience their situations. Their emotions become your emotions and for that reason, you are fully engaged, 100 percent involved. Perhaps you walked away with a slightly different perspective on the subject matter and you remember those experiences because they were almost real. In short, you were entertained, emotionally and intellectually.

so-phis-ti-cat-ed *n.* 1. To make more complex or inclusive; refine.

en-ter-tain *vt.* 1. To hold the interest of, and give pleasure to; divert; amuse. The root word meaning to grab or hold.

Isn't that how it feels when you are involved in a good movie or book? To be entertained is to be drawn into something so deeply and convincingly, that we are fully engaged with all of our senses. We are emotionally committed for that period of time that we are being entertained. And because we are spending some emotional capital, we learn, or acquire knowledge and we remember it. This then, is

EMOTIONALLY CHARGED LEARNING THROUGH SOPHISTICATED ENTERTAINMENT THAT ENGAGES THE SPIRIT AS WELL AS THE INTELLECT

Okay, to be fair, we can also learn something from a boring class, training session, speaker or bad movie if we work hard at it—but not nearly enough, and not even close to the potential of ECL. And if we spend money to transfer knowledge, we most certainly want our people to retain it.

It is therefore not difficult to understand that Emotionally Charged Learning requires EMOTIONALLY CHARGED FACILITATION! Which is exactly what ECL does. By using sophisticated entertainment-industry techniques, ECL engages the learner and improves retention of information, which ultimately produces faster and more sustainable results, IN ANY LEARNING ENVIRONMENT.

Emotionally Charged Learning is the modern world's extension of what our ancestors used to participate in—mythology, and great storytelling. Imagine five or six thousand years ago, before the very first written form of language when people would sit around a fire and tell stories. They were told in such a way that people were completely captivated, which produced heightened emotional responses in the listeners.

Since there was no written language, all knowledge was passed from one generation to the next verbally through a rich tapestry of storytelling. People's very existence depended upon what they learned through these stories and so intrinsically, they all contained a component that allowed various COMPETENCIES TO TRANSFER TO THE WAY THEY LIVED THEIR DAILY LIVES. The net effect of the stories was to teach people how to better themselves and all of society.

Today, of course, we live in the hyper-techno world of knowledge and entertainment. Instead of listening to our elders tell fireside stories, we watch TV, go to movies, go online, play video games and read books. And because the world gravitates toward these media, Emotionally Charged Learning uses them to transfer modern day competencies (learning and applying knowledge), in a compelling, engaging and exhilarating manner.

ECL IS THE MYTHOLOGY OF THE 21ST CENTURY AND BEYOND. It is the way people better themselves and society by enhancing their competency and skills.

In order to more fully understand ECL, it is important to look at the science of emotions and memory and their roles in learning first . . .

PART TWO

THE SCIENCE OF EMOTIONS, MEMORY AND LEARNING

In the last few years, the study of psychology, education and neuroscience have merged and overlapped to reveal that EMOTIONS, ENGAGEMENT, STORYTELLING and ENTERTAINMENT can have a profound effect on memory and learning.

During the 1990s, neuroscientists such as Joseph LeDoux, Antonia Damasio, James McGaugh, and Larry Cahill, among others, worked to uncover the **biologica**l and **chemical** role **emotions** play in **memory** and **learning**. Their work demonstrated that emotions have their own neural pathways, which are mostly at an unconscious level, and they do work to enhance memory and, therefore, learning.

Further, psychologists such as Milton Erickson and Georgi Lozanov have demonstrated the value of placing subjects in emotionally secure states to enhance their suggestibility and, once again, learning. Their work proved that eliciting emotions greatly enhances recognition and retention of information.

Okay, but why entertainment techniques? We have talked about movies and books but what common characteristic do these and other successful forms of entertainment share that make them engaging? It is the same characteristic that makes Emotionally Charged Learning work so well—STORYTELLING. However, not just "telling" a story—it is communicating it in a way that invokes audience involvement. Once you have invested your emotions in a story (or any activity for that matter) you tend to understand and retain that information as opposed to experiences that do not touch your emotions.

Joseph LeDoux, a neuroscientist at the Center for Neural Science at New York University, was the first to discover the pivotal role that the amygdala (uh-mig-duluh), a tiny area in the brain, played in the processing of primary emotions. There is an intricate dance that occurs between the amygdala (primal emotions) and the prefrontal cortex. The amygdala needs the more sophisticated prefrontal cortex to cool its passion, while the cortex needs the amygdala to warm its calculations and to guide it through what matters most deeply to us.

LeDoux said that much of the emotional processing we do occurs at an unconscious level. The emotional system can act independently so that some memories can be formed without any conscious, cognitive participation.

In fact, as science has demonstrated, emotions are at least twice as fast as rational thought. An emotion occurs in less than 12/1,000ths of a second. A cognitive thought takes twice that much time to form, or 24/1,000ths of a second. Though this is a miniscule amount of time, it does demonstrate that emotions occur first, before we have the chance to "think twice," literally. Perhaps there is something to the old adage, "Count to ten before you act."

The neural (independent) shortcut to the amygdala may explain the emotional impressions and memories we experience without being fully aware of their origins. LeDoux referred to this as the "emotional unconscious," a domain of study previously limited to cognitive psychologists. His studies, as well as those of many others, suggest that learning involving emotions occurs unconsciously and independently of conscious cognition.

We often liken the brain to a sort of computer, which would account for the old way of thinking that most learning takes place on a cognitive level. Neurosurgeon, Richard Bergland would beg to differ. He has little doubt that the brain operates more like a gland than a computer. According to Bergland, "The brain not only produces hormones; it bathes in them and depends upon them for proper functioning.

"Intense emotions trigger the release of chemicals such as adrenaline, norepinephrine and vasopressin, which essentially tell the brain—**'Pay attention. This is important. Save it.'**"

The body's reaction to an emotional event has, of course, been hard wired into our genetic code through thousands of years of evolution beginning with Paleolithic Man. His was a harsh environment and he dealt with everything in it on a purely emotional level (not having much brain development at that point in the then short history of man).

Paleolithic Man's primary defense against a threat was his body's innate emotional mechanism of "fight or flight." Not only did the surge of adrenaline and other hormones prepare him to either run or fight; it served as a powerful TEACHING TOOL. It only took one encounter with a wooly mammoth to REMEMBER to run the next time he encountered one.

His emotions served to teach him QUICKLY and THOROUGHLY.

Through evolution, physiologically we have maintained those same instincts. 12/1000ths of a second may have been just enough time to save a life. Today we don't need the more negative reactions of running and/or fighting as a response to a threat (for the most part), but we still utilize the learning benefits of our emotions because, indeed, they still help us to survive, albeit in different and more complex ways.

Evidence that emotions enhance our memories comes from the work of Drs. James McGaugh and Larry Cahill of the University of California at Irvine. These two leading neurobiologists have done research in the role of peripheral hormones like adrenaline in memory formation.

Dr. McGaugh's studies showed that when rats were given a shot of adrenaline right after learning a task, their memory of the situation was greatly enhanced.

During the 1990s, McGaugh and Cahill moved into human studies using drugs and brain scans to find out if their discoveries with rats corresponded to humans. They postulated that . . . .

. . . the memory of emotional situations may be stronger than the memory of non-emotional situations.

To date, McGaugh and Cahill have successfully tested this hypothesis numerous times with human subjects. In one of their experiments, subjects were asked to read a story about a boy riding a bike. One group read a story that was "emotionally arousing" wherein the boy is hit by a car and rushed to a hospital. The other group was given a version of the story that was emotionally neutral. After reading the stories, the group that read the emotionally arousing story remembered far more details than the group that read the neutral version.

Carrying the experiment a step further another group was given the emotional version of the story to read after they received an injection that blocked the flow of adrenaline in their systems. This group could recall about the same amount of detail as the group who read the neutral version of the story. The lack of emotion, in this case the stimulus of their own natural hormones, carried with it a lack of retention.

Cahill and McGaugh also experimented further with emotional learning by having eight volunteers watch either neutral or emotionally arousing film clips. As they watched these clips, their neural activity was mapped using PET scanning techniques. Three weeks later, these subjects took a memory test and, as expected, they remembered the emotionally arousing film clips better than the neutral clips. Notably, the PET scans showed that activity in the amygdala correlated with the number of emotional film clips the subjects remembered. Conversely, activity in the amygdala did not correlate to the number of neutral films they recalled. In other words, the more active that the amygdala was at the time of learning, the more it enhanced the storage of those declarative memories that had emotional content.

A simpler example of Cahill and McGaugh's findings, and one closer to home, can be found during nearly every sporting event. Think back to the time you were watching your favorite team play in a heated rivalry. It could have been anything from an important Little League game that your son was pitching, a soccer game your daughter played in, or The Super Bowl. If it was your favorite team you probably became very emotional as the event unfolded. You cheered, maybe even screamed. You were fully engaged and excited by the drama and, I would guess if you are like me, you not only remembered the final score, you retained all of it; the winning pitch, the missed pass, the bad call by the official; details, details, details. The "movie" of it is probably still vivid in your mind years later and you can play the tape back anytime you choose.

In other words, we remember emotional events more readily and for a greater period of time than events that did not engage us emotionally.

One of the ways we learn is by association with past events. So, it stands to reason that learning that is emotionally charged will be retained longer and used more efficiently.

To further illustrate the power of emotion in memory and learning, a recent study suggests that while both men and women are wired to feel and recall emotions, women have a more keen ability to remember based on emotions.

The study that appeard in the *Proceedings of the National Academy of Sciences,* used magnetic resonance imaging scans of subjects brains that were exposed to various pictures. The outcome demonstrated that women's neural responses to emotional scenes were much more active than the men's. It also showed that women's brains are better organized to perceive and remember emotions.

The study supports the folklore idea that a wife has a truer memory for marital spats than does her husband. One of the reasons for that is that it (the spat) has more MEANING for women and they process it more.

During the study men and women were shown pictures and asked to assign a number from one to three for "not emotionally intense" to "extremely emotionally intense."

While the subjects looked at the pictures, images were being taken of the brains using MRI. The women and men had very different emotional responses to the same photos. For example, when shown a picture of a gun, the men generally assigned a one or two rating, while the women consistently assigned a three (for extremely emotional or intense).

What the subjects didn't know was that they would be asked to return three weeks after the original tests to view the photos again. When they did return, they were shown the same pictures, each for three seconds. In addition more photos that they hadn't previously seen, were mixed in with the originals. They were then asked to choose the pictures that they had previously rated as emotionally intense. For these photos, the men recalled about 60 percent and the women over 75 percent.

Today, self-help gurus challenge us to use our logic instead of our emotions in our decision making process. According to Ruth Palombo Weiss in her book, **Emotion and Learning,** the current obsession to suppress emotions in favor of logical, cognitive thought (at least negative emotions), isn't what it's cracked up to be.

She writes,

"Have you ever been warned not to let your emotions rule your thoughts and actions? Throughout the history of Western civilization there has been a conflict between emotion and thought. General wisdom of the ancients included, 'rule your feelings, lest your feelings rule you.' But recent research conducted by neurologists

and educators shows a strong link between emotion and reason, feelings and thoughts—thereby disproving the adage that emotion is the enemy of reason.

"'I had been advised early in life that sound decisions came from a cool head, that emotions and reason did not mix any more than oil and water,' says neurologist Antonio Damasio.

"He explains that he grew up thinking that reason and emotion were located in separate regions of the brain, each of which had a discrete neural system. He has since discovered that 'reason' may not be as pure as most of us think it is, or wish it were; emotions and feelings may not be intruders in the bastion of reason. They may be enmeshed in its networks, for better or worse."

In her work, Weiss continues to elaborate that emotions are inseparable from the ideas of reward and punishment, pleasure and pain, approach and withdrawal, personal advantage and disadvantage. To have feelings then is to have emotions affect the mind as they occur in the here and now.

The more that science explores the brain's processing, storage and retrieval mechanisms, the more apparent the connection between emotions and reason. Science has discovered that the same areas of the brain that are involved in processing emotions, are also involved in processing memory (more on this in the next section on memory).

In his book, **Life: The Manual**, Dr. Frank Sovinsky discusses this issue:

"The brain is the organ, the mind is its activities, the present, its product. There is remarkable research in the field of neurobiology that is creating fascinating new models of how your brain works. Humankind's curiosity, coupled with the recent advances in medical imaging, have illuminated the shadowy recesses of the brain. Yet, the more we learn, the more questions we have. Just when one riddle is solved another one shows up.

"Research is pushing us back to the future, causing a profound shift in our understanding of how the body and mind function as one. Dianne Connelly was the first to coin the word, Bodymind, to reflect the traditional Chinese medicine beliefs that the body is inseparable from the mind.

EMOTIONALLY CHARGED LEARNING

"In her book, Molecules of Emotion, *Candace Pert, Ph.D., defines our dilemma: 'Emotions are at the nexus between matter and mind, going back and forth between the two and influencing both. Thus, it could be said, that the traditional separation of mental processes, including emotions, from the body is no longer valid.'*

"You experience the world through your bodily senses. These nerve impressions stimulate ancient emotional responses that are shared with every race and culture on this planet. While you are unique, you nevertheless remain a part of the collective family of humankind.

"Whether you are Italian, Native American, Asian, Black or White, you share a common emotional language.

"University of California at Davis professor, Paul Ekman, has confirmed Darwin's theory that humankind has six basic emotions: fear, anger, disgust, sadness, surprise and happiness. In his trans-cultural study, participants were shown photographs of different people with a variety of facial expressions illustrating one of the above emotions. The subjects viewing the photos were monitored with various instruments that would record their physiological responses to the pictures. The results were striking. He concluded that we not only correctly read the emotional expressions of others, we actually react in a profound involuntary way."

The crux of Eckman's findings is very important. It indicates that emotions displayed by others evoke emotions in us. For this reason, one of the most compelling aspects of a good story, especially in a good novel, is not necessarily the great scene descriptions (although those can evoke emotions as well), it is the emotion that we experience vicariously **through the character's actions or thoughts.**

What Professor Eckman continued to discuss was that when you see an expression of surprise on someone's face, you react with some level of emotion. Universally, regardless of race or gender, we are compelled to react from a physiological standpoint. In other words, WE CANNOT HELP OURSELVES.

Great movie directors know this. When they want you to "feel" the intensity of the story, they use a pattern of cuts that invoke an actor's facial expressions and body gestures juxtaposed to what they are thinking. The changes they experience take the audience with them.

We know the character is physically injured, not just by the blood displayed on screen, but by the familiar grimace we can all relate to. The same holds true when a director is trying to convey emotion. A woman biting her lip, brushing her tears away as her lover waves goodbye to her from the departing train, tells us all we need to know about her feelings, more than volumes of copy could ever accomplish.

The physiological responses, as recorded by Eckman's team, showed elevated heart rates, increased blood pressure and even changes in blood sugar levels directly associated with the emotions they saw displayed in the still photographs. Add the music, sound effects, live action and voila! You are being fully engaged.

> *"When an idea wraps itself around an emotional charge, it becomes all the more powerful, all the more profound and all the more memorable. You might forget the day you saw a dead body in the street, but the death of Hamlet haunts you forever."*
> —(McKee, 1997, p. 110)

Dr. Pert, just mentioned in Dr. Sovinsky's book, first came to prominence in the early 1970s for her discovery of the brain's opiate receptor. She describes receptors as "sensing molecules," as microscopic, molecular scanners. Her continuing research has now revealed the molecular basis of the emotions, the tiny peptides that lock into the mind's receptors. But, the resulting molecules of emotion are not confined to the brain. They run every system in your body. Thus, the memories needed for learning are stored in all parts of the body, from the depths of your brain to the tips of your toes.

Whenever new information enters the body, through sight, sound, taste, touch or smell, memory traces are stored not only in the brain, but in the organs and muscles as well. The body is another aspect of our unconscious mind. In addition, the mind and body work as one for filtering, storing, and remembering all essential elements of learning. That is why we remember easiest any information with a high emotional content.

Consider this: if you are over the age of about 50, you are just one of millions of people who can remember exactly where you were and what you were doing the moment they heard the news that President Kennedy was assassinated. Likewise, can you remember where you were at 7:30 AM on September 11, 2001? I can see myself then as vividly as I can right now. I was having a cup of coffee in my hotel room, about to go to an event when the phone rang and a friend simply said, "Eric, turn on the TV. They've blown up the Twin Towers in New York."

> *"There is nothing in the intellect that does not first exist in the senses."*
> —Aristotle

Decision based on emotion is not the exception—it is the rule. Yes, extreme emotions and very negative feelings are not necessarily in our best interests. As with so many other things in life, they are best done in moderation; a middle ground makes sense. For one thing, emotions help to speed up decision making enormously. Emotion is an unconscious biological thermostat. It tells us that DANGERS or OPPORTUNITIES exist.

However, it is important to mention here as well, that **emotion has nothing to do with problem solving, except that it is THE FIRST IMPORTANT STEP IN AN EXTENDED COGNITIVE PATH FROM AWARENESS OF DANGER OR OPPORTUNITY TO SOLUTION AND BEHAVIOR.**

Physiologically, everything we learn first passes through a kind of switching mechanism called the thalamus. It then is routed automatically to various sections of the brain. But first, it must go through the EMOTIONAL stage for the brain to evaluate whether the information is a threat or benign.

As the stimulus or information begins its journey, it travels through a series of feedback loops which originate in long-term memory. Essentially the brain is using stored data to help assess the incoming messages. If the message or stimulus is perceived as a threat, the brain goes automatic in an attempt to process the information through a series of reactions that are both unconscious and conscious. At this point, the brain is trying to decide whether to keep or ignore the incoming information.

When unconscious emotional arousal reaches a certain point, it becomes a conscious feeling, a thought.

Thus, there are some conscious controls in subsequent related cognitive processes. Emotion then activates ATTENTION, our focusing system. The brain quite efficiently then assesses the danger or opportunity and provides useful information. We remember this information and react according to past events, or we recognize that it is new, perhaps a learning opportunity. Many times, this all happens subconsciously.

As Charles Darwin and Dr. Sovinsky theorized, emotions are universal. They also pointed out that there is a direct link between emotions and MOTION, or action. As an example, when mammals are happy, they approach; when angry, they attack; when frightened, they run and when sad, they disengage.

We use our emotions and memory to solve problems or challenges when we react to danger or opportunity. Thus, emotion drives attention, which in turn drives learning, memory, and problem solving behaviors.

This, then, is an extremely important fact:

SCIENCE HAS PROVEN THAT "REAL" LEARNING CANNOT TAKE PLACE UNLESS THERE IS AN EMOTIONAL AROUSAL.

You can be cognizant of a fact or a piece of information, but that does not guarantee that you will remember it, learn from it or retain it.

Though there is disagreement among educators and scientists with regard to the differences in childhood and adult learning, most agree that adult learning is multifaceted.

In adult learning the "emotional" arousal that is needed for learning to take place can be complex. It involves the learner's need to know, their self concept, prior experiences, motivation and their readiness to learn. All of these can be emotional states as well as intellectual considerations.

We will discuss adult learning in more detail later in this book.

Having read to this point about the role that emotion plays in memory and learning, take a moment to think about how you are currently training your people in the knowledge-based economy. How are you investing in your most important assets? Are your training programs giving you a competitive advantage? If you want to make a UNIQUE DIFFERENCE in the marketplace, your employees must make a UNIQUE DIFFERENCE in their job performance. Does their current learning allow them to do this? Is it engaging their emotions not only so they can gain enhanced competencies, but also so they can retain this learning for the long haul? Can you see a tangible return on your training investments?

It is instructive here to note that even when someone is taught or trained, it doesn't necessarily mean that he or she will use the information correctly in a real situation UNLESS IT IS ALSO PRACTICED IN A REAL (or perceivably real) circumstance. This is another way to bring emotion to the learning process and it is one of the reasons why soldiers, police and firefighters are trained using life-like or simulated reality situations. These can range from pilots training in multi-million dollar flight simulators to police training on video consoles, essentially video games and mini-movies.

PART TWO

There are other reasons for using life-like vehicles including:

1. They increase motivation
2. They facilitate the "affective" aspects of learning (those things that describe changes in interest, attitudes and values)
3. They promote interpersonal relations and provide immediate rewards for learning
4. They are at least as effective as conventional techniques in achieving cognitive outcomes (those things dealing withthe recognition or recall of knowledge and the developmentof abilities and skills)
5. They produce improved communication and discussion
6. They tend to produce a more integrated view toward broader sociological concepts
7. They promote individual discovery
8. At the very least, they support and enhance conventional methods of instruction
9. Learning is retained to a deeper level for a longer time

Here is a recent article from *USA Today*, by Marc Saltzman:

"This week, an unlikely exhibitor is unveiling a video game at the Electronic Entertainment Expo in Los Angeles—The U.S. Army.

"America's Army (video game) scheduled for a July release and to be given away free at americasarmy.com, is the first consumer product created by the military and designed to give an accurate depiction of Army life, and to have fun and learn.

"'WE KNOW THAT AMERICANS LOVE THIS TYPE OF ELECTRONIC ENTERTAINMENT,' (sic), says Major, Chris Chambers of the Army's Office of Economic and Manpower Analysis. 'It just made sense that the Army communicate its story where people like to spend time.'

"The game for use with Windows is actually two games in one:

"One is a strategic action game played from a first person perspective where up to 32 players can battle online in a heated military conflict.

"To create graphics that can compete with today's blockbuster titles, Army engineers licensed and modified the leading-edge core programming from other popular games. One unusual aspect is that the person is required to train before joining a unit (online), which includes an obstacle course, rifle range, airborne school, etc.

"The second portion of the game challenges players to set and accomplish varied 'life goals,' such as making money for college, getting married, or becoming an officer.

"'They must make decisions to keep them on their path.' Chambers says. 'Clearly the 18 to 24 male market that plays these types of games might find appeal in something that was authentic.'

"But Rob Smith, Editor in Chief of PC Gamer magazine, says the Army may be trying to target those with technical know-how. 'Modern warfare equipment requires a level of computer savvy that wasn't the case in years gone by. Many game players fit the demographic.'"

Shortly, I will show you how Emotionally Charged Learning uses sophisticated entertainment techniques, coupled with brand leading content, in the appropriate conditions, to deliver meaningful learning that transfers to competency. One of the keys to ensuring this is to understand that when we feel good (positive) while learning, we are far more likely to feel that we did the task (learning, test, etc.) well. And as you may have already guessed, if we feel negative (bored, angry, distracted, etc.) while doing a task, or in a dedicated learning situation, we won't do as well learning or retaining the information.

In Renate Nummela Caine's writings, **Making Connections**: *Teaching and the Human Brain and Education on the Edge of Possibility,* she suggests that we create a sense of surprise and mystery and use humor.

"These techniques foster emotional connections that make a DIRECT biochemical link with memory. Engage learners' confidence. Begin with what they already know because if they are in any way threatened or have a sense of helplessness, their brains will not register a maximum level of input. Furthermore, they won't go beyond what you ask of them. Include meaning by helping learners see how new information connects with what they already know."

As you will discover in part three of this book, this is a crucial element in Emotionally Charged Learning. In, *The Adult Learner* by Malcolm S. Knowles, within the context of the theory of **andragogy** (the concept that children and adults learn differently, and which will be discussed on various levels throughout this book), Ruth Merton, director of the education department, Milwaukee, Y.W.C.A., said that when adults attend classes or are involved in training, unlike children, where the atmosphere is more a "learned teacher-ignorant pupil" relationship, the adult students often possess knowledge and skills that the teacher does not. Because of this fact, there is a need for a spirit of give and take, that induces a feeling of camradeship in learning and the quickest way to achieve this desireable state is through laughter in which all can join.

Stepping aside from emotions just for a moment, let's be clear about what LEARNING is . . .

How do you know when you have learned something? Does learning occur automatically just because you have gained a new knowledge of something you didn't previously have? Or is it only learning when you retain and can recall this newly acquired information, and can continue to recall into the future, and more importantly, put the knowledge to use?

Experts have identified and labeled several ways to learn including "super learning," "accelerated learning," "whole-brain learning" and "integrative learning." Unfortunately, such labels suggest complexity. The best systems are simply "true learning." Better still, they are always "fun." The best systems encourage you to use all your "intelligence" and senses to learn much faster using rhythm, music, pictures, feelings, emotions and action. The best systems are similar to those we used intuitively as infants.

By whatever name, I think you would have to agree that learning only takes place when a person is able to recall and use new information.

In the next section, we will go on to the next building block of ECL: memory and its connection to emotion and learning.

THE IMPORTANCE OF MEMORY

"I'm really afraid of anything that is about losing memory. My fear, of course, is that I would be a shell. In the best-case scenario, I would be just like my dog. Just going moment to moment wagging my tail."
—Bernard Cooper, Memorist

Mr. Cooper may at first sound a bit over-dramatic. However, the fact is, his fear (emotion) probably drives him to enhance his learning opportunities.

REMEMBERING AND FORGETTING ARE THE BASIC PROPELLING DEVICES OF LIFE.

They are the keys to our very existence. Without the written word, stories handed down from generation to generation through sheer memory served the purposes of survival, and the betterment of the individual and society. Memory is, at its root, a survival instinct, the very reason that the body or brain does anything.

In the animal kingdom the sense of smell is an essential survival tool and so animals' olfactory lobes depend upon smell for hunting, sexual drives and the instinct of fight or flight.

All the senses serve as triggers to memory. Each is a powerful key to opening long ago closed doors. There is no telling what sight, smell or sound will unleash a piece of personal history, suddenly making it as vivid and nearly as real as the back of your hand.

Alzheimer's victims have proven to researchers that memory is indeed the propelling and sustaining device of life. In one sad yet illustrative story, we meet a Virginia farmer, Henry Bateman. He is standing next to a cart filled with samples of his herbs. We watch as he pulls out a crisp, neatly folded piece of paper from his pocket. With the other hand he withdraws a pen and makes a notation.

"This is what I carry with me at all times," he says. "These two are now my brain. It is how I remember. It is who I am for the moment. I write things down."

Bateman was diagnosed with Alzheimer's at 57.

"I used to sit while my brain entertained me. Ideas flew about and stories formed and laughter remained . . . now the show is over. Hardly a bard exists in my memory," he says of his condition.

Bateman no longer has a memory, so he must write to save his life. Now he awakens in the dark morning without an awareness of what day it is. He waits for the newspaper or radio to locate him in time. His memory has become so bad, he lives only in the present moment. Once that has passed, the memory of it is gone as well. Not even a smell or a sound from his past conveys any thought or emotion.

There are many factors that determine why we choose to ignore some memories and give importance to others—all of them involve EMOTIONS. A memory from early childhood that sticks is probably associated with a significant event. Perhaps you were in an automobile accident, or you burned your hand badly on an iron. Those are traumatic events, so your brain first filters through short-term memory saying, "Should I remember this?" Traumatic events are automatically associated with a high priority by the brain. However, it takes another step for the brain to memorize something for the long haul.

Short-term memory is essentially a chemical event. Your dog dashes across the street, your heart races for a moment as you look both ways hoping there are no oncoming cars—this memory is automatically chemical and is short term. Within a day, two, or three, it is forgotten. However, if your dog dashes across the street and is hit, two actions take place in the brain. First, as with all memory, it stores the event temporarily as short-term memory and then, if it is more emotional, more important, traumatic, it will be hard-wired. Most likely, you will be able to recall this memory for many, many years. This is accomplished through the cells, which now make new connections to store that memory.

This entire process of storing short-term and long-term memory is similar to how a computer stores memory. The hard drive is where you save important information for a long time. The other space for memory, which is not your hard drive, is where you can dump things.

Ultimately, the brain is wonderful in so many ways as it learns which things will be highlighted and saved and which will be dumped. Think about those seemingly simple tasks both CHEMICAL and BIOLOGICAL. It is what allows us to best move forward in our personal life stories. Imagine all of the things your brain must do every time you do something as simple as walk into a room, every minute detail that is temporarily recorded; the lights, each chair, every sound. Do you really want to remember all of that? In some cases, yes. For example, the next time you enter that room and the lights don't work.

Without memory, we don't have a past. Without a past, we don't have an identity. Without an identity, we are lost; life is chaos.

> YOUR BRAIN IS A MARVEL OF ENGINEERING. ITS CELLS DESIRE ONLY TO SAVE WHAT IS IMPORTANT FOR YOU TO LEARN, SURVIVE, AND ADD VALUE.

It does this most efficiently with emotionally based events in combination with the various forms of intelligence that you possess, to whit:

According to Harvard psychologist Professor Howard Gardner, we all have several different types of "intelligence" and each of us uses them in varying degrees to learn. Others might refer to some of these as "talents."

In no particular order, one is linguistic intelligence: the ability to read, write and communicate with words. Obviously, writers, poets and orators use this intelligence more often than others do (though many people use more than one intelligence almost interchangeably). I know several people who are writers, and are also gifted sculptors or painters, for example. I also know that I learn many things both kinesthetically and visually: through physical movement and watching others or viewing. Discovering this as a youngster, I always knew that I could learn various sports, such as playing football or kick-boxing, literally by watching good athletes in these respective sports intently, and then mimicking their movements myself soon thereafter.

Next is logical or mathematical intelligence: our ability to reason and calculate. Scientists, mathematicians, lawyers and judges would be examples of those individuals who use this type of intelligence the most.

Then there is musical intelligence, spatial and visual, which might be strongest among architects, sculptors, painters and pilots. There is also kinesthetic intelligence, or physical intelligence which athletes, dancers, gymnasts and perhaps surgeons rely on most. And then there is **inter**-personal and **intra**-personal intelligence: the ability to relate to others and introspective intelligence respectively.

If you stop and think about it for a moment you are probably quite aware of which of these types of intelligence you use the most. In **Emotionally Charged Learning all of the intelligences are brought into play in diverse ways.**

In a controlled situation, it is obvious that it would be preferable to teach an individual whatever you wanted him or her to learn by first identifying his or her primary "intelligence," and then use techniques specifically geared to that knowledge. However, in a traditional classroom or any kind of group setting (seminar, lecture), that isn't possible. However, in a one-on-one situation, such as e-learning or tutoring, this is entirely possible.

That is why it is important to understand the role of EMOTIONS in MEMORY. Advances in modern neuroscience research are bringing us closer to quantifying the nexus where emotion, memory and learning meet. Consequently, we are beginning to realize that COGNITION (conscious thought) and EMOTION are not separate processes, but rather are intimately intertwined.

INCREASE MEMORY AND INCREASE INTELLIGENCE

The link between memory and intelligence was studied by Princeton University biologist, Dr. Joe Z. Tsien. He altered genes' receptors and inserted them into the DNA of ordinary mouse embryos, choosing the hypocampus site because that is where memories are initially encoded. The mice born with the new cells were then tested specifically for nerve stimulation. Receptors, which usually remain active for about 100/1,000ths of a second after a stimulation, now remained active for more than twice that time—a subtle but important distinction. Upon further testing, these mice also displayed better memory and greater intelligence. They also learned faster than ordinary mice did.

The reason so much testing is done on mice is because, believe it or not, they share with us a great deal of biological traits, particularly in their memory-encoding mechanism. It is likely that what held true for the mice holds true for humans. Increase memory and you increase intelligence.

This should not come as any big surprise when you think about it. Increased memory capacity leads to easier, quicker accessing of information, as well as an increased ability to associate one thing with another.

DID YOU KNOW YOU CAN BUILD YOUR BRAIN THROUGH EXERCISE JUST LIKE YOUR TRICEPS?

Yes, you can and should exercise your brain just like you do the rest of your body. Of course exercising your brain requires different kinds of weights and aerobics than you use on your body. Brain exercise is the best protection against developing memory disorders and it can certainly make you a great deal more valuable in the workplace. It will ultimately allow you to be happier and could even enhance your standing in society.

Before there were written words, we communicated, survived and bettered ourselves by sharing stories. In order to have any use in the present and for future generations, a great deal of information had to be memorized . . . and accurately. The Homeric epics, *The Odyssey* and *The Iliad*, were RECITED at festivals by entertainers (singers) who marked their rhythm by tapping the ground with staffs. Some scholars even postulate that Homer never even wrote down his poems, preferring to recount them strictly from memory! If you've never read these works, you would be impressed.

Today, of course, technology (in the case of this book that means anything that is an extension of the brain, i.e., pens, computers, tape recorders, etc.) allows us to use our brains less and less. The entire Library of Congress can be stored (essentially memorized for us) on a box of CDs. Like anything else, this is beneficial but also has a downside. Because we can store so much information in so little space and not have to memorize it, our brains tend to become "flabby" if we don't exercise them, not unlike the biceps of a couch potato.

In a knowledge-based economy, where brainpower is the essential asset in all business, you can readily see how important it is to exercise your brain.

"Digging through your memory" is one form of exercise. A friend of mine who is a researcher told me about the first time that she felt she was actually getting smarter—much smarter than she'd ever been before—at the age of 52.

This friend recounted how, while doing research for a book on the various types of intelligence we possess, she was becoming frustrated at her lack of understanding. The person she was researching for was quite intelligent (a Mensa member with an IQ quite a bit higher than hers). My friend told me how she was given specific tasks, information to find and then to assimilate, organize and write conclusions.

After several weeks of struggling, my friend (let's call her Cynthia) was about to give up. She told me she didn't feel she was up to the task. She didn't think she wasn't bright enough to digest the material and then to make sense of it all in her writing. That was until something went off in her brain. I asked her what had happened. She said that while accumulating the research and then having to sort through it and finally, having to make decisions regarding what she was going to write, she found herself literally agonizing over the task of trying to recall facts.

Cynthia's real challenge wasn't so much finding the facts and organizing them, though that certainly required one form of intelligence. It was to make sense of it all and create new information based on what she'd learned previously through association and memory.

She told me that at times, as she was trying to remember a fact or where she'd found it, she could almost feel her brain pulsing. It was not pulsing as in a headache, but as if it were flexing, straining physically to come up with answers. Essentially, that is what it was doing. She was literally "thinking hard." The connections throughout her brain were growing. The dendrites, or branches from the connections, were like roots trying to find water in deep, hard soil. She was trying to associate old and new information. Her memory was allowing her to learn.

Months after her project was completed, she related to me how much smarter she felt. It was like her IQ had literally grown a few points, she said. A year later she told me that that one experience had been so much mental exercise that she now felt all of her thinking processes were stronger and quicker and she had become even better at retaining information. What was truly interesting to me was that while Cynthia reported feeling more intelligent, a year later, she could step back and say that the entire experience had been fun! The challenge of pushing herself beyond her own original perceptions of the boundaries of her intelligence to find that in the end, she felt not only smarter, but more importantly, now felt that there were no limits to what she could learn.

So, it would seem, that Cynthia's increased feelings of "intelligence growth" were directly related to her task of having to "dig through" her recent and older memory. Another example would be that of an actor who instinctively relies on his memories of past emotional events to portray his characters. To understand how a person might act in various emotional scenarios, it is easier for the actor to revisit similar events in his own personal histories to better understand how someone else might respond.

By using her memory, Cynthia, at the age of 52, had made herself smarter. She had literally built more brainpower through a form of exercise.

In his fascinating book, **Mozart's Brain And The Fighter Pilot: Unleashing Your Brain's Potential,** Dr. Richard Restak talks about the emotional aspects of memory.

"No matter how strong or weak your memory for facts, people, and events, there is another aspect of memory that you should seek to enhance. I'm referring here to the associated emotion that accompanies the original experience.

"As an example, imagine that I'm in possession of some pictures of you taken in various situations over the past year (nothing monumental, compromising, or embarrassing; just everyday pictures). Imagine further that I've put these pictures in an album and we are paging through the album together. We're starting with the pictures from yesterday and paging backward to the ones taken a year ago.

"At a certain point in this exercise, you will start to notice a loss of your sense of emotional continuity. In other words, you will experience increasing difficulty in linking your present feelings with the feelings and emotions that existed at the

moment depicted in the picture. Although you recognize yourself and can probably provide some information about what was going on at the time, you're somehow disconnected and unable to re-experience your thoughts and feelings from that past moment. And, isn't that loss of emotional continuity with earlier events too important a part of your memory to relinquish? Indeed, what could be more important than your present ability to recall what was going on emotionally at the time a particular picture was taken?

"*If we allow our emotional memories to disappear, we eventually lose touch with ourselves. If things progress far enough, we encounter a stranger staring back at us from the mirror.*"

Learning Through Emotionally Charged, Sophisticated Entertainment That Engages And Moves The User To Heightened Retention And Increased Competency.

Okay, let's take what we've discussed about emotions and memory and marry that to entertainment to see what happens.

Consider this fact: we are less equipped to experience our world from a physical standpoint (taste, touch, sight, sound, smell) than we are from a mental standpoint. We have more than 100 million sensory receptors that enable us to see, hear, feel, taste and smell our physical world. However, we have TEN-THOUSAND BILLION brain synapses **that allow us to relate new information to store in memories and ideas (mental images)**—to experience things that never actually (physically) occurred to us. In other words, we are much better equipped to understand things (stories, imaginings) that are contained fully in the mind, than we are to learn through our physical senses alone.

Note:
Ten-thousand billion as a number is:
10,000,000,000,000
(memories and ideas).

PART TWO

**Compare that number to:
100,000,000
(one hundred million sensory receptors).**

Entertainment is all around us. It gives us emotional security, a sense of worth and power. Marketing and advertising gurus move us to buy things by entertaining (persuading) us in one way or another. Moviemakers and television producers entertain us with the same visions, as well as the more well meaning altruistic ones. There is a motive in all entertainment and in Emotionally Charged Learning. The motive is to use highly sophisticated entertainment techniques to engage us and to propel us even beyond our conscious knowing, to learn through our emotions.

Most things that are entertaining are also FUN.

And, I would add, one of the very best ways to LEARN just about anything, is by enjoying the process—having fun. Even people who are being ENTERTAINED (scared to death) watching the movie Friday The 13th are having fun.

One aspect of fun is "play," and there are many lessons to learn about the learning process through the study of play. Children and adults approach play quite differently. When children play, they are in fact LIVING THEIR LIVES AND LEARNING SIMULTATNESOUSLY. When children are left to their own devices to play, they begin to make connections and draw conclusions about life (a good reason to let them play more often).

Children left to play often are more likely to become well adjusted adults (and I would argue that adults who truly indulge themselves in play more often, the child-like version, where there is complete abandonment, turn out to be better adjusted adults as well).

Adults need fun, perhaps more than children in many ways.

A recent headline in *USA Today* read, "**Toys bring out the kid in Corporate America.**"

According to the article, the toy industry in a bid to increase income after several years of flat sales, is turning to Corporate America. Their marketing relies on nostalgia as a hook to lure the 40 to 60 somethings to buy such items as a $100 gold-plated Slinky. One newly created division at Lego now sponsors a two-day corporate strategy seminar for executives to use specially designed Lego blocks to help "construct" new strategies (and maybe blow off some creative steam in the process). The cost? $10,000 for a team of 10 executives, and they get to keep the Lego bricks afterwards. (Most executives are just kids in adult clothes).

The rationale for all this is that adults need toys too. Playing with toys can be a form of role modeling, as in being the General, the commander of an Army of plastic soldiers. And it comes as no surprise that the adults favor toys that they remember from their youth. Now, companies that used to want their names on pens, hats and coffee mugs, want Frisbees, Magic 8-balls, Yo-Yos, and Hula Hoops. Etch-A-Sketch is a big item as well. They know that these toys evoke emotions from our past (if you're in your forties or fifties), mental images of a simpler time, perhaps a more pleasant time. A time when you could just play and be yourself.

What originally may have been an almost desperate move into the corporate world by toy manufacturers now appears to be a brilliant idea. They discovered that using play to enhance business is big business.

One executive admitted that he keeps a box of wooden blocks on his desk that he pulls out at least once a week when he's feeling tense. He likes them, he said, because they're like the blocks he played with as a kid. This same executive is working on a management book dealing with business and play based on the concept that there is an acute child in each of us that is dying to come out.

Has learning become boring for you? It happens to all of us. Somewhere along the way, through the "system," a lazy teacher, the search for corporate profits, learning becomes a chore. Can you imagine teaching a four-year old by lecturing him for hours as he sits still in a hard wooden chair? Of course not. Children (and as we will learn soon, adults) learn best by doing, testing, talking, asking, experimenting.

The best and brightest teachers and facilitators are preparing for the challenges of the 21st century by using lessons gleaned from early childhood, i.e.: brain research, SHOW BUSINESS, advertising, television, music, dancing, the movies, sports, art and the electronic media. The single common thread that runs throughout all these resources is a restoration of FUN to the learning process (and as you shall soon read, each of these involves one of the six kinds of intelligence innate in all of us—the six different ways that we learn and relate to the world).

In Southeast Asia, non-accountants learn the principles of accounting through a game. Intel, Apple, Bell Atlantic, Air New Zealand and many other corporations are using games, humor, toys and other techniques to cut staff training time, costs and increase retention of the material. In Japan, telephone linesmen are using music, visualization and games in their training.

In New Zealand, all primary schools use brightly-colored puzzles and games to learn elementary math. Managers from a wide range of businesses are learning in one day how to prepare a complete marketing program using these techniques, most of which fall into the category known as "accelerated learning."

> *"To learn anything fast and effectively, you have to see it, hear it and feel it."*
> —Tony Stockwell
> *Accelerated Learning in Theory and Practice*

Current research shows that all good training and educational programs involve six key principles. For these principles to work best, the

facilitator or teacher must be an *involver,* not a lecturer—one who orchestrates the principles well. These principles involve the following:
1. The setting—being in the best learning situation or mindset
2. The presentation should involve all the senses, be fun, fast-paced and stimulating
3. There must be creative and critical thinking to help process the material internally
4. Ways to access the material through games, skits, and role-playing
5. A way to transfer the learning to real-life applications and connections
6. A regular review and evaluation and also, a way to celebrate what has been learned and applied

It isn't surprising to find that the way these principles work for adults is pretty much the same way they work for children—quickly and easily by exploring and having fun. And they work best when they are Emotionally Charged.

The Power of Mythology and Storytelling

Another important element in the learning mix is storytelling. Contrary to popular perception, mythology did not begin with the Greeks, though they certainly elevated it to new heights. Mythology began with Adam and Eve, or Adam and God (depending upon your viewpoint). As soon as there were two "entities" that could "speak" to each other, there was mythology because simply put, mythology is the transfer of information through the vehicle of storytelling from one person to another, one generation to another, and one culture to another.

Dramatic, compelling stories have been told for centuries as the primary method of "imprinting" and "perpetuating" our values, ethics and morals, as well as our understanding of the world around us. These have been verbal and written. From Adam and Eve, to the Bible, to *Aesop's*

Fables, to *Star Wars*, information and lessons have stood the test of time and stuck in our collective minds.

Scientists say that man has inhabited the earth for more than 25,000 years (in our more modern Homo Sapien state). It wasn't until 5,000 years ago that the first words were even written. This came in the form of baked tablets of clay where the inscribed symbols, known as cuneiform, represented words.

Oddly enough, cuneiform was primarily used for business transactions. The symbols were used first as a means of accounting—keeping track of who owed whom, and how much. However, even after man learned to write with letters and words, storytelling was the preferred vehicle for the transmission of information and it remained that way for thousands of years (I could argue that it still is in many ways). It was always primary to man's survival and a way to better himself and society.

This is how we made use of past experiences, communicated them to others and learned from them without actually undergoing the experiences ourselves. It is for these reasons that humans are naturally aware of stories and are natural storytellers. It is why our intelligence is in large part a "narrative" intelligence.

Most entertainment is a form of storytelling as is good teaching.

As a child your parents probably read to you. You sat on your father's lap as he read aloud the words you could not yet understand and pointed at colorful pictures that were used to illustrate the story. The pictures helped give life to the words, and your father or mother's enthusiasm and perhaps drama, didn't hurt either. As a child you were most likely enthralled with the experience and that is why you demanded that your mother or father read you a story before you went to bed (in addition to being one more way to stay up later). So, much of your earliest learning experiences came in the form of entertainment, which came in the form of storytelling.

If your parents read to you when you were young, like most people raised in that kind of environment, you became an avid reader.

Words are powerful when strung together by talented writers. Rudyard Kipling said, *"Words are, of course, the most powerful drug used by mankind."*

In addition, of course, stories spoken or written are comprised of words. In fact, a complete story can be told in as little as one sentence. Ernest Hemingway is said to have written the shortest short story ever when he wrote this sentence: *"Baby shoes for sale; never used."*

Stop and think about that thought for a moment—though short, the connotation is quite poignant. With only six words, one might conjure up many different stories: A mother loses a child during birth—what to do with all the baby gifts? Perhaps there was a tragic accident, maybe even a murder?

Great leaders are remembered for the things they say, which may be the impetus for change, but it takes powerful words to catapult ideas forward—words so clear and emotional, they carry the enormous weight of vision—of action. Great movies are remembered for their emotion and the words that comprise the dialogue.

Even the most brilliant ideas are short-circuited without the right words to move them out of the simply "aha" stage. Lightweight, predictable words can toss cold water on even the hottest ideas.

Words can be electric, indeed must be, in order to convey any emotional voltage. Even brilliant ideas are short-circuited without the right words, and powerful words in clever and unexpected combinations can bring a brilliant light to even a dim idea.

Words can initiate wars and end them, turn *like* to *love,* make us laugh and cry. Men and women have risked their lives over words. Fortunes have been made and lost and men's honor sorely tested.

However, before there were books filled with words (and even since), the history, customs and culture of a people were passed along to the young by their elders (tribal leaders, grandparents and parents) in the form of stories. Given the complexity and amount of information that was passed along, it is amazing that so much information was so thoroughly retained generation after generation. Amazing, that is, until you realize how emotionally charged the storytelling was. The elders instinctively knew that the stories had to be entertaining in order to be understood and retained, because that is how they remembered their grandparents telling the stories to them. Generally, those telling the stories used music, rhythm, dance and animated physical gestures to add emotion and depth to their stories.

Likewise, political opinions, fiction and science were passed along in the form of stories. We can find examples throughout history. The Greek playwright, Euripides, wrote one of the earliest "antiwar" plays to address the evils of the Peloponnesian war and early British and American fiction writers used the wisdom of biblical texts to promote moral education. Galileo used a fictional and often humorous story in his book, **Dialogue,** to educate the masses about the evidence supporting the sun-centered Copernican theory. In fact, when you think about it,

THE ENTIRE HISTORY OF CIVILIZATION CAN BE SUMMARIZED AS A SERIES OF EFFORTS TO TRANSMIT AND USE INCREASING AMOUNTS OF INFORMATION—stories in one form or another.

Emotions do two things in storytelling: they help to keep us captivated (hold our attention), and they help us to remember or retain the story and many other subtleties within the story.

Writers know this instinctively and they use a range of tools to elicit these reactions including: characters to whom audiences can relate, believable and authentic dialogue, intriguing plots and, of course—tension. How will the hero win? What deserving revenge will be heaped upon the bad guy?

Good writers/storytellers also know that in order for a reader or listener to be fully engaged in the content, he or she must take some "ownership" in the characters. A friend of mine who writes novels related this story to me once:

"Having written only non-fiction for years, I finally decided to write my first novel. After I had finished about fifty pages I asked a good friend (that I knew would be brutally honest about the writing), to read my story and give me her thoughts—for better or worse.

"A week later she announced that she had finished the work and thank God she said she loved it. One character in particular stuck in her mind; the hero, Rocko. I thanked her for her input and told her that I would give her the next installment in a few weeks; she had agreed to read the entire book as I wrote it.

"Beginning the next stage of writing, I was reading back over what I'd given her, and I realized that I had not described the main character very well—at least not physically. All I had included was the fact that he was tall and handsome.

"Being my own worst critic, I decided that wasn't enough. For my readers to really get a sense of this character, I decided I should define him in more detail, which I did extensively.

"Several weeks later, I handed my friend the next 50 pages of the manuscript. Nearly two weeks passed before I heard from her again and I began to worry that she had not liked it, and was afraid to call me with the bad news, so I called her. As it turns out, she had been busy and had just finished it the night before.

"'So, did you like it?' I asked.

"'Yes. I think it's very good, but you've ruined part of it for me?'

"Huh? I thought. 'What part was that?'

"'Rocko. He doesn't look like you've described him. He looks nothing like that. I pictured him with wavy hair, much less muscle bound . . . .'

"As she continued to describe how she had envisioned Rocko, I realized that I had taken something very important away from her—her imagination, or more importantly, her 'ownership' of that character. I immediately rewrote that part of the book and learned a valuable lesson that all good fiction writers know. Part of the fun of reading or listening to a good story is that as we go along we develop the characters in our own mind's eye. We shape them, give them physical and emotional qualities or weaknesses based on the clues that we get from the writer and from deep within our own experiences. This gives us some ownership in the *story and the characters. Without that, we are not nearly as engaged, nor have we spent much emotional capital."*

According to Roger Schank, the former director of the Institute for Learning Sciences at Northwestern University, thinking largely depends on storytelling and story understanding. Most human knowledge and memory is based on stories. He says, "Knowledge is experience and stories, and intelligence is the apt use of experience and the creation and telling of stories. Memory is memory for stories, and the major processes of memory are the creation, storage and retrieval of stories." (Schank, 1995, p 16).

He continues to say, " . . . stories about one's experiences and the experiences of others are the fundamental constituents of human memory, knowledge and social communication. This argument includes three propositions:

1. Virtually all human knowledge is based on stories constructed around past experiences.
2. New experiences are interpreted in terms of old stories.
3. The content of story memories depends on how they are told to others and these reconstituted memories form the basis of the individual's remembered self."

STOP!

Stop for a moment and think about what you just read, especially Schank's third proposition . . . "the content of memories depends on how they are told to others."

Sounds obvious and simple, but the implications are astounding when applied to learning in a knowledge-based economy. How a story is told is directly tied to the memory of that story. That is why EMOTIONALLY

CHARGED LEARNING is rich in its tapestry of visuals, special effects, music, and compelling and engaging dialogue. In a knowledge-based economy, we can not afford to waste time and money on training and information that is not dynamic and memorable. It will not be retained. It will not be utilized because there will be no new competency to transfer to the workplace, so ultimately, it will not benefit the individual or society.

Story-based learning environments can provide engaging worlds where those who learn are actively involved and learn by doing. Story-related activities can promote deep connection-building and meaning-making activities needed for effective learning.

"This approach works because those who are learning are transported and

> *are somehow taken to another place and time in a manner that is so compelling, it seems real. Second, they perform the narrative. Like actors in a play, they are active in drawing inferences and experiencing emotion as if they were somehow real.*
>
> *By adopting a narrative-centered approach to learning, we believe these two characteristics (being transported and performance), can be exploited to great advantage by learning environments.*
>
> —(Gerrig, 1993. As cited by Mott, Callawy, Zettlemoyer, Lee & Lester, 1999, Fall, p 6).

In a modern day application of learning through storytelling, scientists are beginning to understand much more about earthquakes by listening to survivor's stories, some of them hundreds of years old.

If you live in California, as I do, and you've lived here long enough, you will hear the stories told compulsively, reflexively, as part of the local tradition and culture. It's normal to say, "Don't worry, it'll pass in a minute," to terrified visiting relatives as another six-pointer rumbles under and through your house.

Now, the stories that people tell about earthquakes, in centuries-old-villages and in current California cities, are taking on new significance. Seismologists and sociologists and other researchers, who once ignored local lore and myths are turning to the stories in their work.

In one study, Native Americans in Northern California played a part in leading scientists to a blockbuster, evidence of a devastating earthquake in 1700, previously unknown. It turns out it was probably one of the world's largest at an estimated magnitude of nine, in the northwest area of the United States.

In another project, researchers are studying narratives filed online by California residents over the past 10 years, some of which provide striking accounts of big earthquakes. The stories give researchers an idea of how people think and react when the shaking begins.

Scientists in this field are also finding that many of the stories are strikingly similar. Some rely on some of the same enduring literary devices that are used in Emotionally Charged Learning like simple words, vivid mental images and cultural metaphor.

Worldwide, cultures that survive a major disaster typically produce some kind of cultural representation of the event through the exchange of myths and urban legend.

As it turns out, before science stepped in to try and explain the bewildering force of colliding tetonic plates, people told stories to make sense of their world, to share emotions and to pass along what they experienced and learned.

In a different kind of example of the use of storytelling, this time as it relates to entertainment and popular culture, two video game creators decided to build their dream: a massive multi-player online game. Their idea was to develop a game that could be played by up to 10,000 people at a time. Roman Kremlicka and Markus Furhmann, both from Vienna, succeeded and were previewing the game at the recent Electronics Expo at the Los Angeles Convention Center, an annual show designed to overload the senses of both chain-store buyers and gamers looking for a new, totally immersive world to play in.

The two programmers discovered they were right. Apparently, even in the rush to satisfy the 'twitch factor' in video games, they discovered . . .

. . . the story is always the thing.

They found their story line, though simple, was the element that pulled all the noisy, glitzy, pulsating battles together. The interesting thing about humans is that underlying their thirst for the heart pounding, mindless (twitch) content in the games, they love good stories, no matter what.

A story about storytelling

There once was an anthropologist who journeyed to a small village in Western Africa to study how a particular tribe taught their children. As is common of anthropologists, no sooner did he arrive than he immediately began poking around, asking questions and in general watched and made notes.

For the first few days he learned very little of the teaching techniques the elders used. That was until one day he stumbled upon a hut filled with discarded television sets stacked from the dusty dirt floor to the thatched ceiling.

A few years prior, the village had been given the gift of electricity by some well meaning missionaries and, no doubt, some product promotion's representative had supplied them with some essentials including the televisions.

The anthropologist was surprised and confused by the TVs' apparent lack of use, so he approached the chief and asked, "Why don't you use your televisions?"

"We have a storyteller," came the reply.

The anthropologist thought for a moment and said, "That's quaint, but the television knows thousands of stories." To which the chief said, "Yes, but the storyteller knows us."

In other words, the most powerful stories connect with people's emotional essence.

Storytelling possesses something that no media, including books, have and that "something" teachers refer to as CIP, or Contact Interaction Personalization. When you take people on a mental or emotional (teaching) journey through a story, you are given entrée to their hearts and minds through a special door. The listener's inhibitions fall by the wayside. The possibility of failing or appearing stupid is forgotten. The gates of perception are wide open.

Through storytelling people respond more readily to new information through the emotionally charged imagery, unlike what often happens in traditional educational settings. Through storytelling, you are subtly creating a safe way for the listener to journey into his or her own imaginations.

By making an evil character bigger than life or deleting inconsequential boring details, you are responding to your listener's innate emotional needs and interests (CONTACT/INTERACTION).

Essentially, you are also PERSONALIZING by reshaping a story that provides a unique, one-of-a-kind, memorable experience between you and the listener.

Storytelling without words

Technically, a story can be as short as a facial expression. No words are needed to tell us how a young woman in a movie feels when she is told her husband has been killed in battle. Upon silently reading a telegram, we see the piece of paper slip from her fingers and float to the floor as her hands come up to cover her face. Perhaps she weeps, perhaps not, but we know she is grieving. It is written with emotion all over her face, not to mention through her physical gestures; her posture slumps, her knees buckle slightly. Perhaps tears begin to stream down her cheeks.

As quoted earlier, Dr. Frank Sovinsky has pointed out that there are six emotions and they are all unmistakable to another human being, regardless of nationality or race, simply through facial expressions. If we are watching the young woman in the movie, we empathize with her. We know she is in pain, mostly from memory. If we have suffered through the death of a loved one in the past, the woman's grief unearths similar emotions in us because we remember. And even if we have not personally experienced that emotion in the past, we have probably shared a similar situation with a friend who has, and we have some sense of what it must be like.

Such is the power of storytelling even without words. To illustrate this phenomenon further, a recent study by anthropologists of a band of West African chimpanzees is a story of survival using only visuals. Scientists there recently observed one band of chimps using crude stone hammers to crack open nuts, a sophisticated use of tools.

The chimps use carefully selected stones, some of them weighing over 30 lbs. to pound on the tough shell of the panda nut, which contains a high-energy kernel.

The panda nuts are gathered by the chimps when they fall to the ground. However, a thick husk encases the tasty kernel inside and it requires up to a ton of pressure to break open. Yet, if the animals pound too hard, the nut inside shatters and is inedible. What is remarkable to the scientists is that the chimps are controlling the force with a 30-lb. rock, with precisely the force necessary to crack the husk without damaging the nut.

During nut-smashing season, some chimps spend two or three hours a day opening as many as 100 panda nuts. They set up nut cracking stations at strategic hardwood tree roots, which are used as anvils.

This behavior demonstrates a high degree of sophisticated learning because it required the animals to select hammer stones and a distant rock outcropping and then carry them to the anvil. Selection of the stones also requires some thought by the chimps: they have to be flat on one side and heavy enough to smash the nuts and they have to have a place to grasp them.

Mothers teach their children to bang on nuts and some of the younger chimps have been seen hitting nuts with smaller stones, as if practicing. Researchers said this behavior suggests that nut smashing is a cultural, learned behavior, transferred in a non-verbal story.

Today we hear and see our stories more through the vehicles of television, movies and radio—even a 30-second spot on TV is a mini story of one kind or another.

Good stories share a common template—tension. Plots in books and movies usually center on a protagonist (hero) who is trying to achieve a goal. As our hero begins his or her journey toward that goal, tension is subtly, and not so subtly introduced in the form of antagonists (villains) throwing stumbling blocks in front of the hero. As tension increases, and the stakes slowly elevate, the audience is drawn deeper and deeper into the story. The more tension the hero experiences, the more emotionally involved we become, until the conflicts are resolved, the villains banished, or at least they have learned their lessons, and the hero has achieved his or her goal. (Of course if you're the type who enjoys "literary" novels, this formula is probably less important. You are the type who enjoys the way words are strung together, as much as the story itself).

Applying Modern Marketing Techniques
To Entertainment and Learning

So far I have discussed the role of emotions in learning and how emotion effects memory. I have pointed out that in order to learn something, we must first pay attention to it, be made aware of it. Once we have been alerted emotionally, our brain begins to process the information, first through short-term memory (chemical reaction), trying to decide whether to keep it in long-term memory, or pitch it as unimportant. If the information is retained in long-term memory it becomes available at a later time to be experienced again, or to be used as an association in learning something new.

Association is an extremely important aspect of learning. It is inextricably woven with memory. It is where most learning begins. Take the example of a 3 month-old baby. She has very little to associate new experiences to—everything is new, so she struggles along until she can recognize a shape or color or taste. Slowly, over time the child begins to build a reservoir of memories from which to associate new information in an attempt to make sense of the new incoming stimulus. By the time the child is three, she already has thousands of subtle memories to call upon.

EMOTIONS, MEMORY, STORYTELLING, LEARNING

Now, we will add the science and art of marketing, advertising and entertainment to the formula for Emotionally Charged Learning because in today's knowledge/entertainment-based economy, the three are nearly inextricably intertwined in our national psyches and each plays an important role in the learning process. What the marketers and media moguls learned about human behavior, they applied to the art of persuasion (which essentially is another way of teaching). Many of these techniques have been applied to the entertainment world, in particular movies and video games. And, once again, emotions play a vital role.

Contrary to popular belief, people don't think in words or pictures; they think in mental images, which are complex combinations of memories of sight, sound, texture, color, smell, taste, opinion and mood (which is one of the reasons storytelling handed down from generation to generation is so powerful and memorable).

Naïve advertisers typically assume that people are seeing and hearing their ads, but of course, studies prove otherwise. One of the reasons is the sheer amount of messages that we are inundated with on a daily (no wait, an hourly) basis, a heated competition for our attention. Most of this onslaught is not absorbed. In fact very little is retained at all.

A professor of psychology at Harvard, Stephen Kosslyn, recently wrote about *auditory pattern activation* and *encoding*, and how these are essential elements in language skills. Kosslyn tells us, "A word is like a key. When a word unlocks the correct stored memories, it is meaningful."

This is an extremely important statement because it indicates that carefully guided recall of certain stored images is one of the primary paths to learning—hearing and seeing words that have the power to unlock memory.

When good intellectual advertising is pitted against good emotional advertising, emotion will always win out. A good teacher can argue a point with all the intellect at her disposal and not be persuasive.

Playing to the emotions reminds the learner of something he or she has always known or long suspected, or wanted to be true. Emotional content builds on the customer's own experience while subtly persuading with the insertion of a new perspective. As a result of this new perspective, the learner will have new feelings attached to the information they already had. Scientists call this "associative memory." It is one of the reasons, which you will discover in a moment, that after 1955 teenagers in America were never the same again. The messages they received through the media confirmed what they always wanted to be true.

The fact is, we tend to do what FEELS right in most cases then we use logic to justify what our emotions have already decided. After that we tell ourselves that we've made "the intelligent" decision.

The secret of persuasion through entertainment, or through any other medium or discipline, is to use emotion and language that creates a vivid first mental image and closes with the same thing. (Note, I said "mental," not "visual" image). We have spoken already about the combination of sight and sound. Let me add here that the mind does not easily retrieve images of the eye. The mind remembers the images of the mind—mental images that have been placed there by words and emotions, images created by language and pictures using emotion as the prime mover.

In Vance Packard's seminal work, **The Hidden Persuaders**, written in 1958 (and just as valid today), advertising agencies were just beginning to research and understand the role that the subconscious played in people's buying habits. After that, advertising and marketing were never quite the same. Of course, Packard's work centered around marketing and our interests lie in education and training. But how far apart are these two agendas, after all? Isn't all training or teaching trying to "influence" people in a sense—in the sense of changing their behavior? That could be more socially acceptable behavior, or the "buying into" of any new ways of performing (in our case—on the job competency).

With these thoughts in mind, it is instructive to use some of Packard's discoveries. In his work, Packard identifies SEVEN HIDDEN NEEDS. These would apply to learners as well as consumers. They were and still are: a sense of emotional security, reassurance of worth, ego-gratification, creative outlets, a sense of roots, immortality, and a sense of power.

You will note that each of these needs is emotional. There isn't an intellectual "want" on the list. You will also note that in any great corporate environment, meeting these needs or some variation of them, shows up on the top ten list of most employees consistently (remember the Container Corporation story?), even if they aren't overtly stated by employees.

A good example of the research on subliminal persuasion is contained in the book: **Golden State, Golden Youth**. *The California Image in Popular Culture, 1955-1956,* Kirse Granat May.

Golden State is a study that deconstructs the popular culture of postwar America and shows exactly how the "California dream" and the cult of youth came to be linked in powerful and ominous ways. Coincidentally, the study begins with roughly the same period of time that Vance Packard's, **Hidden Persuaders** was being written. It was a time when advertising was just beginning to become a major role in American life, a time when movies were also beginning to be a major mainstream form of entertainment.

Kirse May, a historian, digs into the accumulation of cliché's and conventional wisdom about the California youth culture and reveals how the entire phenomenon can be seen as the handiwork of media driven by the motive of profits, among other things.

These marketers were well aware, even then, of the possibilities of television, music and film to create a model of the "good society." This was the first time in American history when a definable teenage "type" was created. Unfortunately, the idealistic view of a young, adventurous, mobile, carefree and conformist teenager—was almost exclusively white and middle class.

Walt Disney played a crucial role in the invention of this youth culture and the decision to base it in the sunshine state of California was a logical first step. The opening of what later became the prototype for a new form of entertainment—extravagant theme parks, was born out of Disneyland in Anaheim. The opening of Disneyland in 1955 cemented California in the collective consciousness of an entire generation and, indeed, the whole world. Above all, Disneyland elevated the pursuit of happiness from an aspiration to a commodity to be packaged and sold to what May dubbed, "The child imagination market."

It wasn't long before kids were sitting in front of television sets all over the country wearing coonskin caps, watching Davy Crockett or the Mickey Mouse Club after school everyday. Not long after that, one of the original Mouseketeers, Annette Funicello's "Tall Paul," was climbing the record charts and she was staring in teen beach movies along with the likes of Sandra Dee in "Gidget."

The promise of freedom and pleasure, sexual and otherwise was unmistakable, though ultimately as safe and sexless as a Disney cartoon.

That music, those movies, gave the illusion of being daring, but in actuality, there was a lot of teasing with no real payoff. The culture depicted a teenage utopia where there seemed to be no parents or school or church, no legal or government authority, no rich or poor kids and no money problems. The teens of the day, known now as Baby Boomers, bought into it all. They were firmly indoctrinated in the popular culture through media images, marketing, movies and music.

Entertainment played an enormous role in the lives of the "Boomers" who now make up nearly 60 percent of the population of this country. In addition, they have literally defined every decade in which they lived as their culture moved through each one like a collective indomitable force of will. First, it was Rock and Roll and Elvis Presley (the 50s and 60s). Next it was Woodstock, the Pill and the Vietnam War (the 60s and 70s). After that came the "Me" generation of hopeless self-indulgence (the 80s). And in the 90s they made billions in the stock market, then lost most of it in the dot com debacle.

The youth and California phenomenon came full circle ten years after Annette Funicello, with the gubernatorial candidacy of Ronald Reagan in 1966 (who coincidentally hosted the live broadcast of the opening day ceremonies at Disneyland).

He played on the same Disneyesque themes in his own campaign by embracing a safe and wholesome vision of youth. Nearly everywhere he went, he was accompanied on the campaign trail by a bevy of "Reagan Girls," a carefully orchestrated group of young women who wore costumes designed by Nancy Reagan (no waist size larger than 25").

Of course, their presence was meant to cast the golden glow of youth on the aging politician. No studies were ever done, but I would guess the whole charade did not hurt Reagan's bid; after all, he did win.

In both these cases, it would appear that Packard's list of the seven basic emotional needs: a sense of emotional security, reassurance of worth, ego-gratification, creative outlets, a sense of roots, immortality, and a sense of power, were correct.

At about the same time that Packard's work was being digested in the mid 50s, and as Americans were turning increasingly to movies and television and away from newspapers and radio, advertising legend, Leo Burnett's agency was creating visual images to go along with the various products they were advertising. This was the beginning of a concept called "Branding."

Burnett developed what is often referred to as the "Chicago school of advertising." He began to use animated cartoons or characterizations to represent various products. This had never been done before. What was one large canning company's secret name for an experimental pea, "Green Giant," became the familiar, Jolly Green Giant in Burnett's creative hands. Burnett understood that what could have been a boring product, could be made more enticing through this colorful and FUN imagery (the giant), not to mention it could also work as a mnemonic device. (A mnemonic device can be any number of things that help improve memory). In the case of the Jolly Green Giant, it was the lilting ditty (song) that accompanied the end of each commercial. I can still hear that tune in my own mind and I don't believe the spots have aired in more than fifteen years. Ho, ho, ho.

In addition to his initial success, Burnett discovered that his characters had a high recognition factor in many different cultures, not just in America. They became a kind of archetype that could penetrate the psyche in more ways than one.

In nearly every instance of a Burnett creation, the characters and their theme songs (such as Tony the Tiger, Charlie the Tuna and the Marlboro Man) were extremely successful in engaging the audience. They engaged them far beyond what mere "display" ads showing a product with a live announcer, or just a voice-over describing the product, had ever achieved in the past.

Once Burnett's techniques proved successful, of course, brand images expanded to include places as well as characters. Hidden Valley Ranch dressing is one of the more memorable that come to my mind. Then came, "Kodak moments" and periods of time were used as memory devices.

Campbell's soup used the image of a mother nurturing her son on a cold day. Characters, locations and moments became the defining images of American products coupled with memorable music. All of these techniques shared one common heritage.

EACH AND EVERY ONE WAS AN EMOTION BASED FORM OF ENTERTAINMENT.

Like anything that works well, Burnett's ideas began to be practiced by others who also built on those early successes. David Ogilvy was probably the next major figure to come on the scene in the 1960s. He was just as radical in his notions, if not more so, than Burnett. Ogilvey invented the concept of "food in motion," which meant, by his innovative standards, that food should always be shot by a moving camera. He dictated that his ads always "open with fire," which meant that they should start with a very big bang and always be captivating. His use of superimposed phrases and taglines on many ads also helped to drive home his messages.

THE ENTERTAINMENT ECONOMY

Today, nearly 5,000 books are published in this country EVERY MONTH, and all of them, whether fiction or non-fiction tell a story. However, it could be argued that most people enjoy their stories through film or television, or at least enjoy them in a more dramatic fashion.

As with the good books, through the movies we feel a range of emotions: fear, sadness, loss, wonder, excitement, joy and passion. However, unlike books, where we can only imagine how things look and sound, movies convey emotion through a variety of sophisticated entertainment techniques including music, spectacular sets and locations, costumes, sound effects, and an astounding array of special effects including computer generated images as well as animation. The only things missing are the smells and tastes, and I think that was already experimented with.

What is it about entertainment that grabs our attention? What do these and other marketers, moviemakers and television producers know that stimulates us to pay attention? In part, it springs from our biological "orienting response" (once again emotions play a huge role).

This response was first described by Ivan Pavlov in 1927. He described it as our instinctive visual or auditory reaction to any SUDDEN, or NOVEL stimulus. It's part of our evolutionary heritage. Just like our ancestors, Paleolithic Man, we are sensitive to quick movements or stimuli in our environment that are new or unique to us. Of course, surprises to Paleolithic man often meant a predator was lurking about. His senses were extremely acute to surprises; it was often a matter of life or death.

Pavlov rightly discovered that our genes were hard wired for the same type of responses. Typical orientation reactions can include dilation of the pupils, blood vessels to the brain and constriction of blood vessels to the major muscle groups. Alpha waves, the ones that are slow, the ones that relax us are momentarily blocked, at least until the state of arousal or stimulation is complete. During this time of arousal and response, the brain focuses its attention on gathering information while the rest of the body is put into a kind of temporary hibernation.

In the late 1980s, Byron Reeves of Stanford University and Esther Thorson of the University of Missouri and their colleagues conducted studies on the simple features of television. These features included cuts, edits, zooms, pans, sudden noises and those types of techniques that activate the orienting response, which in turn focus attention on the screen. They studied the effect of these activities upon brain waves of those watching television. They concluded that these tricks do absolutely trigger involuntary responses and that their value has a basis in the evolutionary process.

This type of response may partly explain why people say things like: "I don't want to watch as much television as I do, but I can't seem to help it"; "I feel mesmerized when I watch television"; "If a TV is on, I can't keep my eyes off it."

Further research conducted more recently tends to continue to validate these studies. Annie Lang's research team from Indiana University showed that heart rates increase for up to six seconds after an "orienting" stimulus. In advertising, action scenes, music, music videos, these stimuli are produced as rapidly as one per second, effectively activating our responses continuously.

Other studies have investigated whether these types of stimulus affect people's memory of what viewers have seen as well as just catching their attention and manipulating their biological and chemical systems'. In one study, participants watched a program and then tallied a score based on the number of observed changes in "edits," which were considered any change of camera angle in a single visual scene (this is usually accomplished by using more than one camera to shoot a scene). The results showed that retention of the material, or recognition, increased with the frequency of edits, presumably because attention was focused on the screen more than would have been the case if there had been only one camera angle throughout the scene.

Edward R. Guthrie added his *principle of contiguity of cue and response,* to work begun by Pavlov and others. His law of learning, "from which all else about learning is made comprehensible," states that a combination of stimuli which has accompanied a movement, will on its recurrence tend to be followed by that movement. Guthrie placed emphasis on the part played by the learner in selecting the physical stimuli to which it would respond; hence, the *attention* or *scanning* behavior that goes on before *association takes place* became a paramount consideration.

Through these studies and the work of sophisticated marketers, we now know about the impact of color, sound and vivid storytelling. It is fair to say that learning must be emotionally and sensory charged and that entertainment in its various forms is one of the very best vehicles to accomplish meaningful learning.

Emotionally Charged Learning through sophisticated entertainment techniques employs and takes advantage of everything we have been discussing. This includes early marketing techniques developed by Burnett, Ogilvey and other geniuses, studies of the best directors, and research that is being done at this very moment in psychology, learning, biological and chemical sciences and of course, computer technology.

Though ECL is certainly based on decades of research in these areas, in today's media-savvy, entertainment-driven world (TV, movies, radio, music videos, video and computer games, soccer and Little League schedules, books, audio tapes, The Internet, ad-infinitum nearly), our "learned" common sense now easily tells us that individuals are motivated to terminate boring, noxious or aversive stimuli of any kind. Likewise, individuals are motivated to perpetuate and increase the intensity of that which is pleasurable—ESPECIALLY WHEN THAT STIMULI IS KNOWN TO BE A POTENTIAL LEARNING EVENT. Some would argue that humans are quite simple: they move away from pain and toward pleasure, pure and simple.

Based on this hedonistic philosophy and years of research, I propose that individuals are inclined to arrange all of the stimuli in their environment to minimize the time and effort it takes to avert such stimuli. (In other words they move away from pain and toward pleasure). They are inclined to take the time and effort to maximize their gratification (pleasure).

Does ECL take note of this premise? You bet! If learning is to be entertaining, among many other things, it must be pleasurable. It must be fun. It cannot afford to be turned off or averted in any way. We must move away from the pain of traditional teaching or facilitating and toward the pleasure of the new SCIENCE and ART of EMOTIONALLY CHARGED LEARNING. We must be the consummate storytellers, compelling and engaging entertainers and above all, excellent facilitators.

Research into learning through entertainment via the "media" dates back to the 1930s to the Payne Fund studies, one of the first large-scale efforts to investigate media's role in influencing people (Krendl, Ware, Reid & Warren, 1996). The studies' findings supported film's potential as an informal learning instrument. It was determined that film's ability to educate was due to the combination of important qualities in the medium, i.e., wide variation in content, gripping narrative techniques and an appeal to basic human motives and wishes (emotions).

The expansion of television programming and viewing in the mid-twentieth century set the stage for further investigations into how television entertainment affected children. The study emphasized that children do indeed learn from television viewing and then went on to develop the concept of "incidental learning."

Though the viewer's intent is to be entertained, he or she stores up certain information without seeking it and learns in spite of the intentions of the programmers or the viewer.

In recent years, distinguished film producers have intentionally sought to educate the public about important issues through film. Indeed, there is a good deal of evidence that entertainment can encourage an **"adoption of values, beliefs and behavior" across a broad range of topics including such diverse subjects as adult literacy, sexual responsibility among teens, health education and volunteerism** (Rushton, 1982, as cited in Brown & Meeks, 1997 Winter).

Many producers' efforts have resulted in the creation of high quality entertainment that not only attracts awards and recognition for artistic merits, but also has strong viewer appeal. These include such well known films as Richard Attenborough's, *Cry Freedom,* about apartheid in Southern Africa; Michael Apted's, *Gorillas in the Mist,* about preserving the environment; Alan Parker's *Mississippi Burning,* about the Civil Rights movement; Randa Hain's, *Children of a Lesser God,* about overcoming a severe physical disability; Steven Spielberg's, *Schindler's List,* about human compassion in the Holocaust; and Jonathan Demme's, *Philadelphia,* about AIDs in the workplace, among many, many others.

Obviously we live in an entertainment economy, nearly as much as a knowledge-based one. The best form of generating emotions, jogging memory, increasing learning and therefore "action" or "movement" in people is through sophisticated entertainment.

Thinking back now, I can remember quite a few films that moved me quite profoundly and at the same time taught me things I was supposed to have learned in school, but never really did. I remember seeing the movie *Private Ryan* for the first time and how vividly it portrayed the ravages and heartache of war. I wasn't only moved, though, it also gave me a very clear perspective on history; the countries and cities involved, what happened at the Battle of the Bulge and more. These were all things I slept through in High School history classes. I'm sure you can think of a few experiences like mine as well.

> *"Learning is most effective when it's fun."*
> —Peter Kline
> The Everyday Genius

In addition, fun doesn't always mean laughs. If you're the type that likes monster movies or wild roller coaster rides, fun can mean being scared. A friend of mine loves taking long drives on country roads on his Harley Davidson motorcycle, but I've never seen him laughing about it. In short, fun can involve many different emotions.

The simple economics of fun is this: people know what they like. If a product or process is fun, they remember it and will seek it out in the future. To understand the importance of fun in even serious decisions, you needn't look further than Macintosh users continued loyalty even after a series of management blunders and under-performance issues. PCs were more prolific, faster and more powerful, yet die-hard Mac users stuck by their "toy." It was fun to use.

Imagine if all learning was fun. Everyone would be brilliant. Unfortunately, that isn't the case. Scientists have yet to acknowledge fully that the obstacles to learning are not cognitive in nature. It's not that some people cannot learn. It is that they do not want to. We cannot program people to learn as we do with computers. Computers don't need motivation, people do. The current cognitive emphasis on teaching in schools is mimicked in the business world as well and so an essential component of learning is missing in both environments.

There are two forms of motivation—extrinsic (outside, not well connected), and intrinsic (internal). Learning that is entertaining (fun), is intrinsic. Although we need to use both, intrinsic learning is operative when we learn something primarily because we find the task enjoyable and not because it is useful. This is the far more effective and satisfying way to learn just about anything.

Consider the following random facts about learning and entertainment:

- Millions of children have now learned the basics of geography from a CD-ROM game devised by two young Iowa trivia-quiz fans: "Where In The World is Carmen Sandiego?"

- At Simon Guggenheim School, 11-year-old students from the poorest district of Chicago, Illinois have learned to speak fluent Spanish through puppet shows, songs and visualizations.

- In Australia, secondary school students have appeared as French actors in their own videotape production—as a vital part of learning a three-year foreign language course in eight weeks.

- In Liechtenstein, a teacher has created more than 240 games to teach virtually anything—from patent law to geography, history and even physics.

- In Auckland, New Zealand, aspiring Polynesian company managers have learned the main principles of marketing in only 90 minutes playing the Great Pacific Century Marketing Game, with pineapples, bananas and gambling dice.

Mihaly Csikszentmihalyi, learning expert, author and Ph.D., says that when all the characteristics of an enjoyable experience are present, one is in a state of consciousness called a "flow experience." This is a state where people report feeling like they are being carried away by a current, fully engulfed in a separate world of their own temporarily. This results when people are enjoying a game, climbing mountains, playing with babies, reading a book, creating art, or watching a terrific movie.

Emotionally Charged Learning understands these conditions; the things that make people want to learn, read, write, solve problems. One of the techniques of learning through ECL is to empower the individuals to take control of their learning. This is accomplished in many ways: through powerful story telling, engaging content, compelling visuals and sound—immersing them in the symbolic world of the subject matter.

Malcolm Knowles, author of the definitive classic in adult education, **The Adult Learner,** who was considered the father of Androgogy in the United States postulated that there are six principles involved in adult learning. They are:

1. The learner's need to know
2. The self-concept of the learner
3. The prior experience of the learner
4. The relative readiness to learn

5. The orientation to learning and
6. The level of motivation to learn

Of the two forms of motivation, extrinsic would be the understanding of the reward attendant to education. At the corporate level, these are obvious: empowerment, pay raises, bonuses, advancement, etc. Of course, these rewards must be real and evident. In other words, adults are motivated to learn as they experience needs and interests that the learning may satisfy. Other motivating factors that are short term would be: satisfying curiosity, enjoying the content itself, enjoying practicing the skill. Empowerment, pay raises and advancement would come under the longer term motivators.

Intrinsically, the individual must be made aware of how much fun the learning process, especially Emotionally Charged Learning, can be. When learning is fun, when the rewards are obvious, learning becomes its own reward.

Learning through fun and entertainment is known in general as "accelerated learning." There are many variations and applications. However, this type of learning most often involves heightened drama, music, and various forms of visual stimulation. For a glimpse of this learning, you could visit a Leo Wood's chemistry class at Tempe High School in Arizona. Walk into his classroom and the first thing that strikes you are the paintings and photographs on the walls: a Monet, a mountain scene, portraits of Albert Einstein and Linus Pauling, graphics on chemistry and the miracle of life.

From the ceilings hang colorful posters and three-dimensional models of molecules. Baroque music fills the room. In short, the environment is colorful, interesting and relaxing.

Leo Wood uses techniques that were brought to the U.S. by Bulgarian, Dr. Ivan Barzakov, and perfected with his actress partner, Pamela Rand.

Barzakov's techniques were built upon Georgi Lazonov's basic principles, making use of music, visual art and metaphorical stories.

Barzakov's method is called, Optimal Learning, which relies as much on music as visuals. In Wood's class, utilizing Barzakov's methods, everyone is immediately caught up in the drama. He may turn off the lights, turn up a special audio-tape to subliminally stimulate creativity and imagination (alpha waves), and begin to stir up chemical concoctions in test tubes. Suspense mounts in the darkened room as the music continues and sparks of light begin to pop out of the tubes. As the fireworks are going off, Wood begins talking about light and life and their interaction. The sparks become more rapid and of greater intensity. At the same time, the volume of music slowly increases. Wood then introduces them to the subject of the day's learning: life is a miracle and you are part of that miracle.

Walking, still talking, Wood goes to a table where he pours the chemicals into a larger beaker. A giant burst of fire flashes from the beaker and back into the test tube as the music reaches a crescendo. When the lights come on, and Wood is finishing what he is saying, the music stops and the room is dead silent. All eyes are wide open, mouths agape and it seems all of the students are holding their breaths. They are processing what they have just been a part of. The entertainment was so good, they have lost sight of the time and even where they are. As Csikszentmihalyi would say, "They are in flow." In less than 15 minutes, Woods has taught these students about the fusion reactions that occur on the sun. This concept, taught in the traditional manner in nearly any other chemistry class, might have taken hours: accelerated learning.

When tested with an oral quiz at the end of the class, EVERYONE ALWAYS GETS 100 percent. Later exams are also spectacular. Before he introduced these accelerated techniques, 52 percent of the Tempe chemistry students achieved A, B and C grades. Using the new methods they routinely score in the mid 90s.

Wood has managed to motivate his students to the point that they can't wait to learn. His students anticipate new knowledge with the same intensity normally reserved for an upcoming favorite rock concert.

Contrast this thinking with the current typical learning environment in the typical American school as related by Marion Diamond, Ph.D. in his book, ***Magic Trees of the Mind:*** *How to nurture your child's intelligence, creativity and healthy emotions.*

"James Stigler, an educational scholar at the University of California at Los Angeles, has compared the way Japanese and American math teachers operate in their classrooms and has discovered startling differences. (The American approach is familiar to most of us, and encompasses most academic subjects, not just math, Stigler's focus). The American math teacher stands at a podium or near the chalkboard, lectures and demonstrates how to work a particular kind of problem—say, simple one-digit subtraction—then assigns a sample problem for the students to solve in class. After a few minutes, the teacher will lead the class through the problem they just attempted and pose questions about each step in the solution as students try to guess the right answers and say what the teacher wants to hear. The American teacher acts as an authority, a source of knowledge, a supplier of right answers, and a corrector of wrong ones."

This "all too common" approach to teaching is devoid of emotion, engagement, and as the good doctor put it:

"Motivation is itself central to a third explanation for the American education system's relatively poor showing: Many of our traditional teaching methods depend on a child's inner motivation to pay attention and complete assignments. Yet they (the system, teachers), often do little to bolster that inner drive and, in fact, in some ways actively erode it."

It is difficult to be motivated if your teacher doesn't involve you emotionally. One way to do that would be to introduce some fun into the process, particularly with abstract concepts like mathematics, and especially with the young.

Case study: *Learning through entertainment—An effective strategy to promote healthy behaviors.* October 23, 2001: Alejandro Vargas, RN, Peru.

"Communities and small towns in rural Peru enjoy frequent opportunities for social interaction, i.e., Sunday market days, patron saint anniversaries, sports championships, etc. These gatherings are also excellent opportunities to provide health information through ENTERTAINMENT ACTIVITIES.

"A CARE health project was implemented in the provinces of Otuzco and Julcan to decrease child and maternal mortality among its 127,000 habitants (adult literacy is extremely low).

"CARE and the Ministries of Health (MOH) jointly developed "learning through entertainment," activities during these gatherings. Traditional competition games were adapted to provide health information, the MOH staff ran i.e., a "health education roulette". Additionally, drama, song and dance contests were organized during these social gatherings.

"Groups of volunteers assisted in the performance of drama plays, and popular songs and dances—all with health messages. Popular radio stations during peak hour's broadcast winning performances. The results? Exit interviews demonstrated huge improvements in knowledge and attitudes towards key healthy behaviors. In combination with other project interventions, "learning through entertainment," increased health-related knowledge and practices among families. For example, the percent of mothers who recognized two danger signs during pregnancy increased from 4 percent (1996), to 51 percent (2000) and the percent of newborns who received breastfeeding within the first hour of delivery increased from 26 percent (1996) to 57 percent (2000)."

One of the important aspects of learning through play, fun or entertainment is that the individual has the opportunity to discover for himself. If learning is to be done through a sophisticated form of storytelling, then the individual must be free to "invent."

When we read a well-written novel, if the writer has allowed us to discover on our own ("showing" us rather than "telling" us), we tend to invent the characters and places in our mind the way that we choose to see them. In so doing, we take some ownership. We are fully engaged.

The economics of learning through fun and entertainment are simple. Entertainment as a stand-alone experience or as content added to other products speaks directly to the emotions. If a given product or process engages me, does its job and is fun, I am going to choose it over another option that doesn't.

The Role of Music in Learning

The fact that music has the power to change and elicit our moods is well known. Each of us can probably remember a time when we've selected a particular tune to help us feel more energized or happy, or to calm us. Good news! Science supports this idea.

Carol Krumhansl of Cornell University found that music with a quick tempo brought about all the physical changes associated with happiness in listeners. In contrast, a slow tempo in a minor key (as in the blues) led to sadness.

Recent PET imaging studies by Robert Zatorre and Anne Blood at McGill University substantiates Krumhansl's findings. (www.sciam.com/explorations/2001/-122-1music/index.html).

Studies linking improved learning with music listening first came to the public's attention through the research of Frances Rauscher and her colleagues at the University of California's Center for the Neurobiology of Learning and Memory in Irvine.

In one of their studies, 36 undergraduates scored eight to nine points higher on a spatial IQ test after listening to ten minutes of Mozart's "Sonata for Two Pianos in D Major." Although the effect lasted only ten to fifteen minutes, the research team found the relationship between the music and spatial reasoning to be statistically more significant compared to other students who used relaxation and silence instead of music (Rauscher, Shaw & Ky, 1993).

Sound is a powerful portion of the learning process whether that is music or conversations and dialogue. Were you aware that separate organs do not only receive sight and sound, but also store and process it? Did you know that more of the brain is devoted to sound than to sight? Does it surprise you to learn that the portion of the brain that stores the memory of sound touches more areas of the brain than any other? Is it any wonder that those who create movies spend so much time with the sound tracks and the way that words are spoken on screen?

Visual *images* are processed in the brain's visual cortex, which is located at the base of the skull. Just above that, in the back of your head, is the visual association area where visual *memories* are stored. Sound is processed in the auditory cortex, just above your ear, and your *memory* of sound is stored in the auditory association area, which occupies most of the sides of your head. Here is where words and sounds are stored.

Bear with me just a moment longer.

The tiny place where your auditory and visual associations meet is a spot called Wernicke's area where objects are named. When you imagine in your mind's eye a purple lion, for instance, it's Wernicke's area that attaches the words "purple lion" to that image. Therefore, Wernicke is the prince of nouns.

Now, in an area of your auditory association there is a spot called "Broca's area," which is a powerful extension of auditory association into the motor association cortex. The motor association cortex is the center of ALL PHYSICAL ACTION and Broca's area is the center of action words.

This is where verbs are generated, sentences adroitly constructed and the area that enthusiastically anticipates what others are about to say.

One of the objectives of Emotionally Charged Learning is to influence these areas and the prefrontal cortex, which is located just across from the motor association cortex, right behind your forehead . . . AND THE SHORTEST LEAP TO IT IS FROM BROCA'S AREA.

Vision and "vision words" happen at the back of the skull. Action and "action words" happen at the front, in Broca's area, right next to the prefrontal cortex. The EAR is strategically located right in the middle, THE KEY TO EVERYTHING.

In ECL, we describe what we want the listener to see and they see it. We cause him or her to IMAGINE taking the action we would like to see him or her take—and they take it!

Contrary to popular belief, people remember more when they HEAR something than they do when they SEE it without accompanying sound. Actually, the human brain does not understand the written word until it has been translated into the spoken word IN THE MIND. The two types of memory associated with this phenomenon are called echoic memory, or sound retention, and iconic memory, or image retention. Echoic is auditory and iconic is visual.

Either way, echoic or iconic memory increases with repetition and each does better in combination with the other. In other words, hearing is superior, but hearing AND seeing together repetitively is the best. Seeing alone, is the weakest, but in combination with hearing and the other senses, it is also one of the best forms of learning.

> *"Engage the imagination, then take it where you will. Where the mind has repeatedly journeyed, the body will surely follow. People go only to places they have already been in their minds."*
>
> —Roy H. Williams
> from *The Wizards Seventh Law of the Advertising Universe*

PART TWO

More on music . . .

Millions of school children have learned a language with more than 500,000 words built from just 26 letters. They learned the English alphabet or their ABCs by singing and rhyming them to a little ditty. A, B, C, D, E, F, G, H, I j k, elemenopee . . . .

I spoke earlier about the importance of learning by combining sound and visuals through entertainment to increase retention of learned information. Consider this fact: To learn faster, you must first slow down the brain. One of your brain's "wavelengths" is most efficient for inspiration, another for sleep and yet another for being fully awake and conscious. Studies have now revealed that a fourth brainwave is the most efficient "frequency" for learning in the most effective and efficient way. It is what some call the "alpha state."

Dozens of research projects have found that music is a very efficient dial to tune into the frequency. They have found that in a special kind of relaxation, which music can induce, your brain is the most receptive to new information. That state has been referred to as "relaxed alertness" or relaxed awareness.

Most of what we know in this field can be traced back to pioneering research started in the 1950s by Bulgarian psychiatrist and educator, Georgi Lozanov. Lozanov originally set out to discover why some people have "super" memories. After many years of research, he concluded that we all have an "optimal learning state." This receptive state occurs when heartbeat, breathing and brainwaves are all synchronized. The body is then relaxed, but the mind is concentrated and ready to receive new information.

We now know that people can achieve the ideal learning state easily by initiating deep breathing and listening to music with a very specific slow tempo in the 50 to 70 beats per minute range. The most common music in this range is that of the 17th and 18th century Italian composers, Corelli and Vivaldi, France's Coupertain and Germany's Bach and Handel.

In his studies, Lazanov found baroque music harmonizes the body and brain by unlocking the EMOTIONAL key to a super memory; the brain's limbic system. This system processes emotions and is the link between the conscious and subconscious brain.

MUSIC IS LIKE THE FREEWAY TO THE MEMORY SYSTEM

Today, teachers trained in the use of baroque music for learning are particularly fond of Vivaldi's "Four Seasons." Most of these teachers also use specially prepared videotapes in their teaching sessions using soothing word-pictures to match the music and encourage relaxation.

In general, the left side of your brain plays a major role in processing logic, words, mathematics and sequence—the so-called academic parts of learning. The right side deals with rhyme, music, pictures and daydreaming, or the "creative" activities.

Sounds simple, but of course it isn't. The left and right halves of your brain are linked by the "corpus callosum" which is a complex switching system of 300 million neurons. The corpus callosum constantly balances the incoming messages linking abstract impressions with concrete, logical messages.

Here is an example of how different aspects of the brain work together in an integrated way through entertainment. If you're listening to a song, the left brain would be processing the words and the right brain would be processing the music. Therefore, it is no accident that we learn the popular songs easily because the left and right brains are both involved—and so is the emotional center of the brain in the limbic system.

The Visual Aspects of Learning

We have spoken about the power of storytelling, learning with and without language and I have discussed the use of music. This is an interesting

PART TWO

story that illustrates the use of comic book visuals and stories as a vehicle to learn.

From the Associated Press-May 10, 2002.

"Minneapolis—Is Spiderman's web strong enough to support him as he swings from building to building?

"Why did Superman's home planet of Krypton explode? How much would the Flash need to eat in order to run around the globe in 80 seconds?

"The man to ask is University of Minnesota physics professor, Jim Kakalios. He is entering his second semester teaching an elective course for freshmen called Science in Comic Books, in which he uses the stories and illustrations contained in comic books to stimulate learning.

"Kakalios says that using comic books to teach the fundamentals of physics is a great way to stimulate his students. 'It seems by the time they left the class, they were looking at the world with a more critical and more scientific eye,' he says.

"The fun lies in pointing out where the comic book writers got the science right and where they got it wrong. Kakalios, a comic book lover, came up with the idea for his class after applying physics to a 1973 Spiderman comic in which Peter Parker's girlfriend, Gwen Stacy, dies. Gwen is knocked from a bridge by the evil Green Goblin, but Spiderman catches her with his webbing an instant before she hits the water. When Spiderman pulls her up, he discovers to his horror, that she is dead.

"Spidey was shocked, but Kakalios wasn't. The professor estimated Gwen's falling velocity, applied Newton's Second Law of Motion and calculated the G-forces exerted when she went from 95 mph to a standstill in an instant. "It's not surprising her neck broke," Kakalios says.

"'The explosion of Krypton is one of those cases in which the comic book writers got the physics right,' Kakalios says. 'In the early Superman comics, the explanation for his superpowers was that he came from a planet whose gravity was much greater than Earth's,' says Kakalios. 'Thus a hero so strong that he could leap a tall building in a single bound.'

"Kakalios calculated Krypton's gravity by working backward from the force required to leap a building on Earth. From there, he concluded that Superman's planet must have had a core of super-dense, and dangerously unstable materials. 'Then you realize why Krypton exploded,' he says.

"For his final exam, Kakalios had students choose a comic book scenario to work as a physics problem. Kristin Barieri tried to figure out how much caloric energy the Flash would need to circle the globe in 80 seconds, as he did in one comic book. She concluded that the superhero simply could not have eaten enough to do it.

"'He would have been able to get the first burst of energy, but he would have sunk in an ocean after that,' Barbieri says."

The Role of Television & Movies in Learning

Every single day more than **3-1/2 billion hours** is spent watching television. Scientists argue about this enormous expenditure of time (some would say a waste, as in "vast wasteland"). Some stress that viewing involves a transfer of valuable information that enriches our store of knowledge. Others contend that television provides viewers with much needed entertainment, relaxation and escape. The debate rages on. My personal opinion is that television has the ability to do all of these things—facilitate learning, entertain and waste time. Like any other opportunity, it depends upon how you use it. The more important point though is that it is an irrefutable and integral part of the lives of Americans, and to some extent, people the world over. It is not going to go away.

Because it has become such a potent part of our lives, we have become conditioned to it and other visual forms of learning and entertainment that are similar, i.e., movies, videos, video games, etc. Computer terminals and the Internet have successfully mimicked this form to a great extent. Now with the advent of high-speed digital sources of transmission (which will no doubt continue to move information at even increased rates of speed), we are able to watch streaming videos online as sharp and clear as television and movies.

If we think of anything that produces changes in consciousness—a perception, a sensation, an emotion, thought, memory, as a stimulus, then all stimuli contribute bits of information to a person's consciousness in one form or another.

However, as we discussed earlier, for information to become meaningful, signs must pass through our ATTENTION (short-term chemical-based memory) for filtering, before it is passed along for permanent storage. If you do not pay attention, then these various stimuli cease to have much value. Attention, then, is a general resource for cognitive processing. The importance of attention can not be overestimated. Without attention to focus us mentally and an attendant program of priorities, we don't learn, communicate, or adapt very well.

As we learned in the section on marketing and advertising techniques, a great deal of research has been conducted and applied to this entire subject of capturing and keeping the attention of television viewers. Everything from music and sudden noises, to subtle camera angle changes including cuts, edits, zooms, pans, and those types of techniques activate the **orienting response**, which in turn focuses attention on the screen.

Emotionally Charged Learning uses all of these techniques in combination with storytelling and sound to produce vivid and engaging learning experiences.

Today the one thing that hundreds upon hundreds of millions of people have in common, aside from their humanity, is TELEVISION. It has become the dominant form of leisure and the most powerful form of mass communication ever known. In just 80 years TV has become the primary vehicle for information shared by the world.

What is it that makes this electronic box so compelling, so hypnotizing and so entertaining? It combines nearly every form of learning that we use. It captivates us through our sensory neurons: sight, sound, even *feel* if your bass is big enough. We watch it. We read it. We listen to it . . . perhaps one day we will smell it.

By way of the orienting response devices, through the viewer's *attention*, by *association*, into his senses and then ultimately connecting to his emotions through vivid (sometimes) storytelling, the pictures, music and messages radiate out and through us. How can we not be hooked? (At least on good programming).

We can visit far away exotic places and people without ever leaving the comfort of our *Lazy Boys.* Simply by tapping a button on a remote, we can see, hear and practically taste just about any subject matter we could wish for through hundreds upon hundreds of channel options. In short, through television, movies and to a lesser extent books, we live vicariously. Subconsciously we long to have our imaginations stretched. We crave stimulation. We want and need the release from our sometimes mundane or stressful daily lives.

More Americans now have television sets than have refrigerators or indoor plumbing. The medium has become an institution, altering, influencing and persuading every person and organization in this country and many others across the globe (remember the story of the African tribe and the televisions stored in their huts?).

At any given moment on any evening of the week, fully one third of the U.S. population is watching television. In the winter that figure jumps to 50 percent! The only activity that takes up more of our time is sleeping and working. On average an American spends about eight hours sleeping, five to eight hours watching television (or at least having it on) and at least eight hours at work.

Today, being entertained is a cultural value among consumers. THEY EXPECT IT, indeed demand it. It's treated as their entitlement and they feel shortchanged when they don't get it. If you doubt this just watch what happens in the typical household when they are watching their favorite program and the dish or cable goes on the fritz in the middle of the show.

In Robert Kubey and Mihaly Csikszentmihalyi's book, ***Television And the Quality of Life***, in criticizing the medium, they site the informal work of a former advertising executive (of all things), Jerry Mander (1978).

"In what he deemed were the most frequent terms used in ordinary conversation and correspondence to describe how people felt about television viewing. His list reveals a prevalent set of beliefs about what happens to people when they watch TV:

"'I feel hypnotized when I watch television.' 'Television sucks my energy.' 'I feel like it is brainwashing me.' 'Television spaces me out.' 'Television is an addiction and I'm an addict.'

"More than a few research subjects have reported that the television set is a dominating presence whose power they can not easily resist. Some of the most compelling evidence of this phenomenon is anecdotal. Take, for example, these remarks from Mander's collection: 'If a television is on, I just can't keep my eyes off it' and 'I don't want to watch as much as I do but I can't help it. It makes me watch it.'

"During a radio talk program, social psychologist Milton Resenberg (1978), recounted his experience with television in this way:

"'When I've got television on in my home and I have to get up for one of the conventional reasons . . . I feel temporarily unfulfilled, even if I don't really want to see what's on the set. Some part of the total sensory experience has suddenly been subtracted and I'm left in some slight state of tension until I can turn my gaze back to the screen.'

"And one final example:

"When psychologist and survey researcher Percy Tannenbaum (1980), has written:

"'Among life's more embarrassing moments have been countless occasions when I'm engaged in conversation in a room wile a TV set is on, and I cannot for

the life of me stop from periodically glancing over to the screen. This occurs not only during dull conversations, but during reasonably interesting ones just as well. Judging from the behavior of the people with whom I was talking at the time and from reports of friends, and colleagues, I am far from alone in this behavior and its accompanying chagrin. (p.112).'

"These representations of the power of TV to attract attention and the viewing state and its effects compel us to ask what it is about the interaction of people with television that causes such phenomena?"

(Is there an echo in here?)

Television—It's life in a bottle. Who wouldn't want to watch?

IS IT ANY WONDER THEN THAT EMOTIONALLY CHARGED LEARNING COMES TO US FROM ANOTHER FORM OF TELEVISION—A COMPUTER MONITOR?

When engaging people through vivid storytelling and sophisticated entertainment, it makes no sense to conduct learning through any other medium, if we are to reach them where they are most comfortable, fully relaxed and attentive. Besides, it isn't nearly as easy to change the channel.

Movies came before television, but not by much. People were already demonstrating an affinity for the movies even before there were "talkies." Before Al Jolson spoke his first words to a stunned theater audience, people were in love with silent pictures (with subtitles and an organ player nestled in some far corner of the theater providing drama through background music).

Even without subtitles, much of the story could be discerned through the emotions and actions of the actors. It wasn't long after Jolson's black and white talkie, "The Jazz Singer," that the cinema experience incorporated color for the first time. After that, we were off to the races. Sound effects eventually incorporated stereo, then sophisticated surround sound that was digitally enhanced. Color by Technicolor was all the rage and even 3-D had its brief, but entertaining hey-day.

One enhancement after another greeted theater audiences who were hungry for more action, pathos and special effects in their storytelling. Originally, animation was used only for the cartoons that preceded the main attractions and then animation became a source of entertainment as full-length stand alone features themselves. Eventually this technology as well became enhanced and when movie makers got their hands on computers, animation began to blend into live action to the point where today, it is nearly impossible to tell the computer generated images from the filmed real versions. (See *Pearl Harbor*).

Animation has become a huge Hollywood business, even though for many years Disney and others nearly abandoned the art because of the costly nature of using human artists to painstakingly illustrate thousands upon thousands of vinyl cells for even one relatively simple scene. The computer remedied that. Now (2002), animated films such as, *The Final Fantasy,* are astounding in their illusions of reality. The human face (emotion) was until recently nearly impossible to duplicate to this level. Now computers that do a billion calculations per second make these types of films possible. And, there seems to be no end to the appetite of audiences for just about any form of good movie making entertainment.

In another section of this book I discussed the importance of mythology and storytelling going back to the first conversation (story) between Adam and God. Movies, like the myths they are built upon, are attempts to explain, in an indirect, poetic and metaphoric way, the purpose and place of humans. Like the earliest myths, humankind, through movies and television, continues to attempt to answer timeless questions: Who are we? How did we get here? Where are we going? Where will we go (if anywhere) when we die? How are we supposed to behave? How can we relate to the great forces of life and death? etc., etc., etc.

EMOTIONALLY CHARGED LEARNING

All of these questions are an attempt to learn through storytelling.

In his book **Myth & Movies**, Stuart Voytilla is able to identify various movie themes and story lines and then tie them to specific myths. Some of his comparisons include:

The Mythic Structures of Action Adventure: *The Treasure Of The Sierra Madre, Seven Samurai, Raiders of the Lost Ark* and *Die Hard*.

The Mythic Structures of Horror: *Invasion of the Body Snatchers, Jaws, Halloween, The Fly* and *Silence of The Lambs,* among many others.

Each of Voytilla's many in-depth examinations are fascinating as he traces ancient myths and stories from the earliest times as the basis for nearly every movie ever shown. Screenwriters looking for ideas would be well served by reading his book. It would seem there is nothing new under the sun, only new ways of telling it when it comes to stories.

PART THREE

THE BUSINESS OF LEARNING
THE CASE FOR E-LEARNING
USING DIGITAL TECHNOLOGY
TO <u>E</u>NHANCE LEARNING

Today, we live in the first era of human evolution where it is possible for EVERY SINGLE PERSON ON THE PLANET TO COMMUNICATE WITH EVERY OTHER PERSON ON THE PLANET INSTANTANEOUSLY (albeit one at a time or in small groups) . . . with voice and live, real time action.

The Internet computer revolution has shaped more of our lives than the combined effects of the first printing press, the automobile, radio, and television! Isn't that astounding? R. Buckminster was indeed right . . . smaller, faster, bigger, smaller, faster, bigger, etc. etc.

The older generation that Tom Brokaw talked about in this book, **The Greatest Generation**, grew up with television. This generation has grown up with television *and* the computer. The young have become fully acculturated through the Internet, and now they are beginning to demand that the Internet be entertaining. They are quite adept at multi-tasking their entertainment as well. While they are watching television, there is a CD playing in the background and the eyes are going between the TV and the computer screen as they surf the Internet. Will they learn on the Internet? Most definitely. Will they also want to be entertained simultaneously? Emphatically, yes.

I haven't a nano-doubt (about a billionth of a second) that those individuals and companies who do not take advantage of this technology will be severely developmentally disadvantaged.

Singapore comes closest to being the first country in the world to leverage this technology as a nation. As early as 1986, Singapore was creating its National Information Technology Plan, aimed at creating the first fully networked SOCIETY, where every single home, school, office, business and government agency would be connected through an electronic grid.

In 1997, they outlined their master plan to spend almost $1.5 billion U.S. in the following five years to introduce the world's best interactive information technology to its school system. By the year 2003, Singapore's 450,000 students will share at least one computer for every two youngsters. All of its schools are already linked to the Internet.

In addition, the government has encouraged more than 3,000 international companies to locate on its tiny city state peninsula.

Even more important though, the digital revolution is forcing a complete rethinking of teaching and learning methods.

MORE THAN 10,000 ARTICLES ARE PUBLISHED ***EVERY DAY*** IN SCIENCE ALONE (which while astounding is nevertheless a very good thing).

Unfortunately, so much is published, it is impossible for any teacher to even read a fraction of the output, let alone master the details and teach it to their students. So, where does that put the traditional role of the teacher and the learner?

People can learn nearly anything if they have access to the information and are allowed to learn through their own unique style with their own personal strengths.

E-learning stands for <u>E</u>lectronic, <u>E</u>nhanced and <u>E</u>ntertainment learning. Call it the E-Factor. Enhanced online learning means that it's not just entertainment driven—content is king as well. It must be fresh, provocative, engaging and intelligent.

Some people learn by reading quietly by themselves. Others learn better in groups. Some study sitting in chairs, lounging in bed, listening to music, reading or moving physically. But guess what the one common thread is that runs through all learning experiences?

IT IS EMOTION!

We all learn best through our emotions, through *mental* imaging, which combines the power of sound and sight, smell, taste, tactile, non-tactile (or at least the perception of those senses being used) . . . .ALL EMOTIONAL.

Because we know this and because we have this wonderful technology of the Internet and instant communications, it is now possible for everyone on earth to learn the same thing, at the same time, through the same medium, but in a different way. Everyone can learn in a way that is customized to their personal learning styles, time frames, physical locality. EQUAL BUT DIFFERENT learning opportunities.

There is a confluence of factors that are responsible for the rise in e-learning including some we have already talked about, such as the accepted recognition that human capital is the cornerstone of the new economy and central to your company's ability to innovate.

In addition, there has been a huge influx of capital and important participants into the e-learning marketplace. It can no longer be denied that the reach, consistency and sophistication of the Internet make e-learning a natural vehicle for training. In fact, now that we make fewer things, have fewer factories and the majority of employers have a fewer than 25 employees (anytime, anywhere) workplace, our training and education must parallel these realities. And it can through Emotionally Charged e-learning, by taking advantage of instant access, universal access, virtual collaboration and complete learner control.

In the theory of andragogy, we have discussed in several places in this book, espoused by Malcolm Knowles, it is thought that adults have a deep need to be self-directing and that individual differences among people increase with age. E-learning appeals to both of these needs. Online learning takes place when the learner is ready, willing and able and it caters to individuality through the sheer nature of the delivery vehicle.

E-learning is most definitely here to stay and to evolve quickly. It is more than just a name change for training. It bears on perceptions of what we do, how we do it, and the valuations of companies.

In Dr. Frank Sovinsky's book, **Life: The Manual**, he states,

"According to new research, technical expertise is only half of what's required to be successful. Studies conducted by the University of Washington and the University of Michigan showed that people who succeed in high tech, high stress jobs, have common sub-conscious (emotional) traits that enable them to thrive under pressure.

"Hard knowledge of technologies may be less important for those looking to rise to the top of their fields than 'soft' skills—intuition, the ability to process a lot of information, and decisiveness.

"'Specific technical know-how isn't as important as a good measure of EMOTIONAL INTELLIGENCE AND INTUITION,' says Jon Carter, a recruiter at Egon Zehnder International in Palo Alto, California . . . 'The ones whose personal contributions save the company from disaster are those who bring grounded or factual intuition to bear on the job, people who can assimilate large amounts of data in a very analytical way, and can synthesize it, and then step back and let their intuition kick in, can have what it takes to be successful and help their companies do the same.'"

Now all we have to do is apply all this to your company's needs and structure through what I call Unified Learning, a combination of live and online-based learning through emotions and entertainment.

The new millennium will bring us even more choices than we already have (a staggering thought). There will be increased possibilities for accessing information, for travel—both real and virtual—all offering thrilling new challenges and opportunities—and all offering monumental chances to waste time and money as well.

On the one hand, it is undeniable that the Internet gives us a wider choice of sources of information and undoubtedly in the decade to come even more. But . . .

. . . INFORMATION IS **NOT** KNOWLEDGE.

Information is but another stimulus, an attention-getter, a resource. Unless it is understood, retained and utilized, it is just data. By reading this book you hopefully have a better understanding of what knowledge really is and of course its importance. Without emotion, the placing of events, people and feelings into an increasingly complex and idiosyncratic context is but an avalanche of information, which is no better than one of snow.

The Internet bombarding us with more information will not increase our wisdom. Smart companies are not heading into a future where simply amassing facts becomes more important than developing individual and collective understanding and knowledge.

All of this is why we must be selective with technology. There are many resources online. The real task is to sort through it all for those opportunities that offer the highest quality learning experiences we can possibly find. We can ill afford to waste our assets (our people and their time), on experiments that don't work.

Individuals and teachers are discovering that digital technologies add a much-needed dimension to the teaching and learning of emotional intelligence in teaching the core subjects. The flexibility of new digital tools provides corporations and facilitators with an avenue for creativity and exploration in just about any area of learning.

In particular, online learning through the Internet allows individuals to learn interactively at their own pace, in whatever environment is most comfortable and efficient for them, i.e., at work, in the evening or weekend, at home or on the road, not to mention the issue of privacy. In short, as stated above, the learner is IN CONTROL.

In a manner of speaking, online learning that is exciting, fun, compelling, and engaging, and is ECL based, is a form of simulation as much as a flight simulator or the U.S. Army's new computer game mentioned in the beginning of this book.

The experts say that if you can teach someone through simulation to master the complexity of flying a 747, you can teach them how to be a better manager. Mention the word "simulator," however, and the mind races to visualize multi-million dollar equipment to train pilots. The challenge then to both the developers of simulation software for "soft skills" and the public perception is that it's tough to envision such a product.

For some developers the products are modeled after TV and video and for others they're computer games. More important than the medium, though, is the art and science of teaching. In terms of computerized and online simulations for learning, they can be reduced to three stages: reference, application and remedy. Within that template, a simulation could be performed with a pen and piece of paper. But wouldn't it be far better to use 3D graphics, movies, animation, movie stars, great storytelling (dialogue, plots, surprises, music), a unique set of problems, leading edge content that is all structured to be as "real life" as possible. We are working now working on a program called "Life" that will do just that.

In appearance, at least, the vehicle (a computer monitor) and the content (video movies, stories, etc.) of online learning are similar to television. (We've already talked about the positive aspects of learning through a familiar medium). At least for a little while longer, for all their power, television and the movies are still one-way mediums. The Internet, in contrast, is two-way and can be extremely interactive, at least when it comes to Emotionally Charged Learning.

When web based digital technology is married to highly sophisticated and relevant Emotionally Charged Learning, the results can be startling. Applied properly, ECL results in an exciting, more enjoyable, faster and easier way to learn while retaining far greater content than traditional learning experiences.

Today's online technologies using high-speed data transmission, sophisticated video looping, coupled with a wide range of sound enhancements, makes it possible to present extremely high quality visual and sound experiences online. In the case of Emotionally Charged Learning, this means Hollywood quality movies consistent with what today's "movie and TV" influenced consumers expect.

This means the first exciting, passionate, personalized learning experience for the corporate consumer.

When people go to a movie or watch a show on TV, they expect to experience a wide range of emotions. They want to laugh, cry, and be scared, feel empathy and be excited. Emotionally Charged Learning is on the leading edge in this regard. Today's corporate learner can experience the same range of emotions, while retaining significantly increased amounts of information. This results in a higher level of learning and a greater transfer of competency applied from the learning to the workplace.

Quick Facts:

E-learning is more efficient than the typical classroom.
Studies show that it takes anywhere from 25 percent to 60 percent less time to convey the same amount of instruction in a classroom setting. Time is money.

Delivery is uniform.
In a hypothetical classroom setting, to train 1,000 people, placing 30 at a time in classrooms for five-day sessions with one instructor will take more than eight months for all of the students to complete the course. By the time half of the students are finished, the material will have changed, or been updated or the company might have gone on to other priorities. One of two things can happen in this scenario. Either half the students never get trained or half of them will have received different instructions.

In an effort to shorten training cycles, extra instructors can be added. However, that presents similar problems: different teachers with different styles and different content. In both situations content is not consistent.

With e-learning, everyone can learn the same thing, at the same time in their own way. New knowledge is rolled out to everyone instantaneously. And, if it's Emotionally Charged Learning, the rewards (increased productivity) to the learner and the company are nearly as rapid.

These are some examples of current use of online technology. Recently the Pennsylvania Department of Environmental Protection used an integrated online system that replaced their outdated system of inspections and levying fines, which has freed up time to allow them to pursue their real mission—protecting the environment.

Enterprise Rent-A-Car now uses an automated system to streamline the cumbersome replacement rental process.

The Michigan Department of Transportation has automated its collection of inspection data and cut the costs of building roads and bridges utilizing an online system.

Dow Chemical recently mandated that all 40,000 employees within 70 countries take and pass an online course on workplace respect and responsibility. In addition to being cost prohibitive, it might not have even been possible without a Web-based training system.

In another Dow online program on safety, the company saved $6 million, safety incidents have declined as a result even as Dow's emplyee baes has grown 25 percent.

RETENTION AND PERFORMANCE—TRANSFER

Until recently, employees were taught through classroom attendance, textbooks and manuals, one to one hands on demonstrations and more recently, online. Like being captive to a dull teacher in a classroom or an even duller textbook, e-learning and other "innovative" initiatives that fail to ENGAGE learners through their emotions, in an entertaining manner, have been and will continue to be INEFFECTIVE.

Many experts feel that 75 percent of educational software (secondary grades through high school) does not teach much at all. And I would agree. Drill and kill software is among the most popular being purchased by schools, yet it is the least educational. These kinds of programs interpret correct answers and then increase the difficulty, but don't allow time for the student to absorb the material. And, of course, in this scenario, there is absolutely no attempt to be engaging, entertaining or to touch any emotional cords.

Edutainment is a word that was coined in 1991 when school teacher, Jan Davidson's, once fledgling teaching center began to explode into overdrive. Beginning with a single $3,000 Apple II computer and with a friend, she began writing programs to drill students in vocabulary and mathematics. The introduction in 1991 of entertainment to the learning mix sent their once tiny business off the charts. In 1994, she and her husband Bob offered Davidson & Associates up as a public company and in 1996, they sold it for nearly **$1 billion!**

A better example of a software program that could be more closely identified with "edutainment" would be Lightspan. This software package is used by many school districts. It utilizes vivid animations and loveable characters that lead children toward a more engaging experience. Still, this software could not be considered emotionally CHARGED, though it is emotionally based at least.

Though a large part of ECL is online based, there is a vast difference in ECL and traditional e-learning. The promise of e-learning is tremendous. It is reusable, anytime, anywhere, just-in-time training that is irresistible. Unfortunately, until just recently, e-learners knew this was not the reality. Large numbers of students are bailing out of e-learning. The inability to keep learners engaged sufficiently so that they do not shut off their computers and fail to benefit from the great promise that e-learning brings, is the biggest challenge we face in this arena.

Emotionally Charged Learning was designed to specifically address this issue by captivating people's attention. By combining proven powerful and sophisticated entertainment industry techniques through hip, culturally vogue scenarios (stories), ECL turns ordinary training into an ongoing, emotion-filled learning experience.

However, the ultimate goal of any training is for the learners to use their newly gained knowledge (competencies) in their work. This process is commonly referred to as "transfer." It begins with an individual's motivation to use the new set of skills and knowledge and moves through initial attempts to use them through stages of regular implementation.

Increasingly, how much you know is less important than how you solve problems (as discussed in Dr. Sovinsky's example). As we also discussed, simulations, or life-like training, are the preferred way to measure intellectual skills. Traditionally they are characterized by multiple, interrelated events that present real-world problems to solve. Orientation to learning is one of the key premises of adult learning processes. In contrast to children's and youths' subject-centered orientation to learning, adults are "life-centered" (or task-centered or problem-centered) in their orientation to learning.

Adults are motivated to learn to the extent that they perceive that learning will help them perform tasks or deal with problems that they confront in their own lives. They learn new knowledge, skills, values and attitudes most effectively WHEN THEY ARE PRESENTED IN THE CONTEXT OF APPLICATION TO REAL-LIFE SITUATIONS.

Emotionally Charged e-learning incorporates these techniques to not only increase knowledge, but to develop problem solving capabilities in learners.

In truth, training of any kind is simply a means to an end. In the case of ECL, the end is a dramatic change in the behavior of the learner on the job. Simply put, "transfer" is the cumulative effect of being presented with emotionally charged information scenarios, learning (getting it), retaining that new knowledge and then immediately applying it in a way that creates value.

Ruth Colvin Clark, author of numerous articles and books on building effective training, addresses this transfer effect in detail in her book, *Building Exptertise.* To enhance the transfer effect in situations that require judgment and adaptation of knowledge to each job situation (known as far-transfer training), Clark (1999) advocates using a "schema"-based training design, providing varied context and examples and teaching related process-based knowledge. The value of this approach is that it develops the learner's "schemata" which are storage structures for knowledge and built in long-term memory. In the following excerpted paragraph, Clark explains how this process works:

"As one develops expertise in a domain, the relevant features of each experience become abstracted into the growing schema. When encountering a new situation, the individual maps it by analogy into the appropriate existing schema. The schema, in turn, activates relevant solution procedures. To build expertise, the instructional program must help the learner generate robust schema that will be activated by real world problems and that embed the appropriate solution procedures to solve these problems."

Inherent to ECL is the use of this approach. The stories that the learner views, hears and experiences are based on contextualized, relevant and varied job-related problems which build upon and expand the learner's knowledge map or schemata.

There are three closely related areas of cognitive psychological research that help to explain how prior experience influences learning: schema theory, information processing, and memory research.

Schema are the cognitive structures that are built as learning and experiences accumulate and are packaged into memory. In other words, we all have our own set of schema that reflect our experiences and in turn become the basis for learning new information.

The schema theory is related to mental models. A relatively new strategy that many organizations are embracing, particularly those that are involved with Emotionally Charged Learning, is called "Learning Organizations." A Learning Organization is one that learns collectively and powerfully and is in a constant trasformation process to better collect, manage and use knowledge for corporate success. Mental models (related to schema theory) are considered one of the five core characteristics of Learning Organizations.

Mental models are deeply held internal images of how the world works, images that limit us to familiar ways of thinking and acting.

In terms of processing information, prior knowledge acts as a filter to learning through attentional proccesses. In other words, learners are more likley to pay more attention to learning that fits with prior knowledge schema and less attention to that which does not fit.

This is also why ECL is an entertainment based process. Since most have us have been raised in an entertainment environment (television, movies, videos, music, etc.), it stands to reason that these vehicles fit the internal images, or mental models (schema), we have of how the world works.

PROFITABILITY AND ROI

Assuming your company is similar to many, your single largest cost of doing business is your payroll and the subsequent benefits provided and paid for, to help retain your "people." In other words, your employees' BRAINS are the costliest part of your operations, but they CAN also be the best investment. It, therefore, makes perfectly obvious sense to invest in continuing education and training to insure your people are always on the cutting edge.

In the **100 Best Companies To Work For in America,** nearly every company listed has pioneered new forms of staff involvement: partnerships, stockholding, profit-sharing, CONTINUING EDUCATION, job-sharing, flextime, project teams and many other innovations. Most of these new ways of working were demanded from the workforce, in addition to health care benefits, vacation, sick leave, work-at-home programs, maternity leave (for wife and husband), free daycare facilities, and more to come.

Everyone is involved in sharing the profits. In fact, you cannot work for some companies unless you own stock. If you can't afford to buy their stock, they will lend you the money interest free because it is essential to them that you have literal ownership of the product or service.

These same types of companies pay for many kinds of education and not only the kinds that further the company's cause in the marketplace, but also those that nourish personal growth.

The very nature of the knowledge-based economy we live in dictates a new nature of education and learning systems to prepare us for the future (which, by the way, is tomorrow morning around 6 a.m.).

The new methods of education and learning require increasing investments there as well. We wouldn't think of starting a fire in the fireplace tonight by rubbing two sticks together, yet most of what passes for education and training is based on concepts nearly as old as flint and fire.

"There is a significant push that's going on from corporate America that's looking at training as a strategic weapon and a competitive necessity. We believe the Internet will democratize education and training by increasing access, lowering the cost and ultimately improving quality and efficiency. In the old economy, training was a COST CENTER. Today it is the #1 SOURCE OF COMPETITIVE ADVANTAGE. Training's necessity has gone from just-in-case, to just-in-time."

—Michael Moe, CFA
Director of Global Growth
Research, Merrill Lynch

Traditionally, learning environments and situations are judged by effectiveness (transfer). Effectiveness is defined as how much information is retained and then applied. This effectiveness can be measured through testing and through observation of the application of the new knowledge, and of course through ROI.

Several case studies that follow shortly will serve as some real world examples using ROI. In addition, there is the long and established literature on ROI, led by the distinguished work of Jack Philips, Scott Parry and others. I would be hard pressed to improve upon their work.

Aside from the fact that there is already an abundance of information on ROI, a strictly ROI approach almost always focuses on COST REDUCTION AND AVOIDANCE. And as I've said at least three times in this book, human capital can no longer be considered just a cost. It is the most important investment you can make in today's knowledge-based economy. Granted, investments must show a return just as any other cost of doing business.

As long as we're on that subject of reduction and avoidance, let me ask you a couple of simple questions. How much money did your company waste last year sending employees to far away seminars, conventions, classrooms? Did some of them spend more time around the pool or in the casinos than they did learning anything meaningful? (Of course some of them did). Now remember, when computing the costs, you not only have to add up the tuition, plane fares, lodging, food, and other obvious expenses. You also have to try to determine WHAT IT COST YOU TO HAVE THOSE EMPLOYEES LEARN NOTHING? What is the cost of having them learn nothing while your competitors stay home, save tons of money and get smarter and smarter day by day, in every way?

Perhaps a better question might be: "What is the highest and best use of our training dollars?" The only honest answer is another question: "How do you plan to measure success?" Everyone wants to make money, a name and/or a difference. What is important is how we prioritize these wants. There is no right or wrong here, though how you allocate your priorities can have a dramatic impact on your bottom line. Therefore, the real question is not, "What is the best use of the money?" Rather you should ask, "What do I most want to make—money, a name, a difference—or all three?"

The approach used with ECL optimizes the employee's ability to grasp, synthesize and apply the knowledge presented to his or her job performance. And beyond effectively transferring knowledge to job performance, today's business decision makers are looking for training solutions that show a strong return on investment (ROI), a way of doing a cost-benefit analysis. So, for the benefit of those who prefer ROI, here are some examples as relates to e-learning in general.

For training and e-learning, ROI becomes the net cash benefit from a program divided by the cost of the program (Phillips, Phillips & Zuniga, 2000, 2nd quarter). One of the great advantages to e-learning is that it readily lends to easy tracking of courses and measurement and hence to determining the training ROI.

Marc Rosenberg, an international authority in performance improvement, conducted a cost analysis comparing e-learning with traditional classroom delivery for two hypothetical companies in his book *e-Learning*. In his analysis, one of the companies, a large scale organization that trained 30,000 people over three years, realized a savings of $6.64 million (Rosenberg, 2001 p.218, table 8.2). The second company, a small-scale organization that trained 500 people during one year, also realized significant savings of $660,000 (0. 219, table 8.3).

Recent reports from industry also demonstrate the cost savings that can occur with e-learning. NCR, KPMG Peat Marwick, Microsoft, PNC Bank, Bellsouth, IBM and GE are a few of the companies reporting on cost savings that can be directly attributed to e-learning, largely a result of preserving learner productivity and reducing travel costs.

Case studies showing cost savings with e-learning:

1. Dave Siefert, Director of NCR University Of Virtual Learning, reported on a recent cost-benefit analysis of all types of technology-oriented training. The analysis was based on a survey of 288 employees and

showed that web-based training delivered nine times the benefits versus the costs in terms of productivity and the quality of experience (Berry, 1999, November). KPMG Peat Marwick is just beginning to transfer training to the web. Douglas Stefanko, National Director of Consulting, Training and Development, estimated that online training costs *one-sixth of what classroom delivery runs.*

2. Diane Oswell, Assistant VP Global Human Resources and Development, Microsoft, places the cost of delivering MS Excel technical support course at $150 to $300 per user. *The comparable cost on the web is $2.50 (Berry, 1999 November).*
3. Beginning in 1998, PNC Bank set out to convert up to 70 percent of all training to online delivery. As of June 2000, 40 percent was online. "Training costs—primarily involving physical facilities, travel costs, printing and instructor time—have decreased approximately 25 percent compared to 1999." (Cases in online learning: PNC Bank, p.78. 2000, September).

4. Bellsouth's Wireless Group is moving to 100 percent web-managed curriculum for new hires. "Training costs will decrease by 75 percent compared to 1999, with savings related primarily to physical facilities, travel costs, printing and instructor time. Bellsouth also anticipates reduction in first-year turnover and improvement in revenue-per-transaction in the first 120 days." (Cases in online learning: Bellsouth, p.78. September, 2000)

5. IBM estimates that for every 1,000,000 classroom days converted to e-learning, more than $400,000 can be saved. For 1999, the company expects 30 percent of its internal training materials will be delivered online, with anticipated savings of more than $120 million. (Business Week, 1999, p. EB34, as cited in Rosenberg, 2001, p. 219).

6. After analyzing the efficiency of an orientation course, GE decided to implement an online version of the training. Afterwards, GE conducted an ROI of the online course and found that employees were able to learn the same amount in three hours as in the onsite course, which took three days. GE was able to reduce the number of productivity hours lost and save on travel and living expenses. In addition, they no longer needed to spend the money upgrading the training facility, which would have cost $4.5 million (*Worthen,* Feb. 15).

(And these examples are just specific to "online" learning in general. I can only imagine how much better their results would be if they married their training to ECL techniques in addition to getting their training online. More on that in a moment).

In one of many case studies specific to e-learning, conducted by Toni Hodges, ASTD Research, 2000, he says:

"Bell Atlantic used a product knowledge training program to compare self-paced, computer based training, and multimedia (slides, videos, television), training effectiveness on performance and sales."

A control group was used to isolate the effects of the training program from other influencing factors. Pre-and post-surveys and pre-and post-tests were administered to the participants. Other sources of data included customer call observations and actual sales of the products introduced in the training program.

What was the bottom line?

- Knowledge training scores were higher for the groups receiving the training program than for the control group.

- Scores were not significantly different within a month of the three groups receiving the training through different methods
- Those receiving training through computer based techniques scored higher on knowledge tests than those participating in the paper-based training.
- Those receiving training through multimedia scored higher on knowledge tests than the paper-based and CBT participants.

ROI was performed on the three forms of training interventions and these were the results:

Paper based ROI= 100 percent
CBT ROI= 1,592.3 percent
Multimedia ROI= 2,059.8 percent

What does all this tell us in a nutshell? It tells us, at least in this case, which is a specific example of e-learning, that KNOWLEDGE, TEST RESULTS and ROI were higher using computer based training than paper-based. The same held true for the results of training conducted using multimedia techniques, only more so.

NOW IMAGINE USING BOTH COMPUTER-BASED AND MULTIMEDIA TECHNIQUES ALL IN ONE APPLICATION AND THEN THROWING IN HIGHLY CHARGED EMOTIONALLY ENGAGING CONTENT.

In his study, Hodges concluded the following:

- From this study, you can see how ROI fits into the evaluation of e-learning. You can observe how ROI is useful in measuring the difference between traditional learning and two forms of e-learning solutions. The figures provide you with raw data to present to others in your organization.

• ROI fits into the evaluation of e-learning programs the same way it fits into the traditional programs. The same procedures are followed regardless of the delivery approach.

• ROI should be considered in evaluating the effectiveness of e-learning solutions.

• Conducting an ROI can help you provide bottom-line information on your training programs to senior management.

You can see we must go beyond simple cost savings due to reduced travel and increased worker productivity. To show the complete ROI story, we must take a broader view. In one ROI study, Greg Wang, Director of Strategic Management for DPT Consulting, worked with a large financial company that had a high turnover rate (Worthen, 2001, February 15). Most left because they were dissatisfied with the level of training. To address this, the company implemented a skills development program. The ROI result they wanted was a decrease in turnover that would represent savings greater than the cost of training.

In fact, measuring ROI is tricky since evidence of the "return" may be more difficult to measure financially. As Rosenburg states:

" . . . while it is true that better leadership in the firm can reduce employee turnover, the investment in leadership training may be more compelling because of the company's conviction that better leaders are more open and forward-thinking about the impact of change on the company. Very hard to measure, but

certainly a worthwhile goal—one that shouldn't be abandoned because a specific ROI could not be calculated."

It could be argued then that companies should be looking at more than just the ROI. Rosenberg (2001) suggests that they should also ask themselves questions such as, "Are we a smarter, more insightful company as a result of this investment? How has learning impacted our customers? What effect has learning had on employee retention, morale, etc.?"

A recent article in *CIO Magazine* discussed a new system used by Dow Chemical executives. They restructured their company around business processes rather than location. Since they are scattered over the globe an intranet-based HR system was designed to serve their employees. As part of the system, Learn@dow.now, a $1.3 million e-learning module they now deliver standardized training around the globe. During the first year, the program delivered a cost benefit of $30 million, which included savings on training delivery, class materials and salaries. All employees were required to learn how to use the system and to sign up for the first classes.

In Michael Napoliello's groundbreaking guerilla marketing book, **Big Bangs For the Bucks**, he addresses the often-murky waters of ROI in this manner:

"Since Big Bang thinking often incorporates nontraditional promotion and marketing techniques, measurement is not as easy and not as exact as many marketers would like. This is often the reason that Big Bang techniques are avoided and marketers fail to follow their gut instincts, i.e., 'I know it's the right thing to do but I just don't know how to prove it.' This is where many of the Fortune 500 marketers leave themselves open to attack from the little guys—the entrepreneurial marketers who follow their gut feelings and don't feel the need to measure and analyze everything to death. This is how aggressive guerilla marketers really get in touch with consumers, break new ground, establish new products or new brands and steal market share from the big guys."

In the short term, e-learning in almost any form will result in cost savings, but we should also be examining the quality of the learning experience, because it speaks to the broader questions that Rosenberg poses.

ECL provides this quality e-learning. It is achieved by using entertaining and emotionally engaging stories to create intrinsically motivating learning environments. Stories can facilitate natural learning, and perhaps most importantly, the stories that are used, are based on relevant job-oriented experiences which work to help individuals grasp, process and transfer new knowledge in their job performance.

Think about it in this fashion: How many of your employees do you think are giving you 100 percent? There is such a thing as "discretionary energy" (having more energy than you need to get by on). I have found that by motivating people through the appropriate and intelligent use of reward and recognition, among other things, they will give you some or all of their "discretionary energy." Quality learning is its own reward. This is the most cost-effective way to increase productivity in the company that I can think of. It is, without a doubt, the most powerful weapon in business in North America and, it's also the most underutilized.

One dramatically easy way to convince your people to give you more of their discretionary energy is through the education/ development.

This is just one of the many distinct advantages of using ECL. If you will recall, in the very beginning of this book I spoke about some of the compelling experiences I have had while learning. These were the examples:

- Were you ever enthralled with a college professor's ability to both entertain and teach you? Did you look forward to his or her class more than any other?

- Did you ever learn something that was so exciting, you set the alarm extra early so you would get to work before anyone else and experiment with the new knowledge?

- Have you ever learned something new and compelling from a movie or a book, so much so that it was almost like an epiphany?

Wouldn't it be great to achieve this in the workplace? I know you can readily see how this type of learning experience can energize your people and give them a reason to give you some of that discretionary energy. It is so exciting to learn and just as exciting to apply that new knowledge. How you reward your people after that is up to you.

But I can promise you this: It will be the most cost-effective, exciting and productive INVESTMENT that you will ever make in the history of your company.

FOR THOSE CEOs, EXECUTIVES AND LEADERS WHO WISH TO LOOK BEYOND ROI . . .

. . . what are some other techniques for measuring training effectiveness? How about basing the benefits and returns of e-learning and ECL on the CREATION OF VALUE? This can be addressed by using three models:

An overall evaluation model that looks at "business results" and the "creation of value" through a broader, and in my opinion, more telling view, of educational effectiveness.

The second model would be more like traditional ROI in that it would look at the financials, the cost reductions and avoidances. Call this the financial model.

A third way is a model that scrutinizes "value creation," or ways that an organization improves, innovates and "competes." (Remember: technology is not compassionate, sympathetic or gentle. It crashes into existing systems with a take-no-prisoners approach, while it simultaneously destroys them, creating new ones in its wake. You can get crushed trying to stop it. Step out of the way or surf the powerful waves of change to wonderful new worlds).

Each of these three techniques or approaches are necessary and symbiotic to a full understanding of the benefits, costs and value of ECL and e-learning.

The Overall Evaluation Model

When comparing cost reduction or avoidance in the traditional sense, and assuming that does occur with e-learning and ECL, it is also important to ask another obvious question: What happens if no learning took place or if the people taking the training found it to be irrelevant to their job? These are things you will obviously want to know. Without putting the effectiveness of the training under the microscope, the numbers have no real meaning. It would also be helpful to know if some significant percentage of the learners did not complete the program. For these reasons and others, it is important to use an overall evaluation of the training to view it in the larger context of "educational effectiveness."

In the overall evaluation model or technique, you would apply 9 criteria. They are briefly:

1. **Use**-
Was it used, and if so, was it used as intended?

2. **Course response**-
These are questionnaires designed to provide insight into the effectiveness of the structure and content of the material. It is important that

there is a balance between open-ended and forced-response questions in the material, as is the case in ECL.

3. **Relevance-**

   Are the learners highly motivated by the structure and content? Are they excited to begin applying these new ideas to their jobs? It is obviously important to know if this is occurring, or if the learners secretly consider the material a "joke."

4. **The creation of value-**

   The kind of leaders that can not only surf the Tsunami wave of change and innovation, but can "hang ten," so to speak (are so good they are perpetually in the "zone"), know that cost reductions and avoidance can only take them so far and last so long. They are valuable tools, but only the obvious ones in the first drawer of a multi-drawer tool chest.

   The creation of value criteria is all about improving the TOP LINE, not avoiding the potential horrors of the bottom. CEOs that apply this kind of criteria are the same ones that dwell on beating competitors and obsess about their capacity to innovate and respond. They know that these are the seeds of growth and shareholder value.

5. **Intellectual skills-**

   I spoke about the importance of measuring the ability to solve problems, as well as how much you know, as a result of your training. Once again, simulations are the preferred way to measure these skills. Based upon learner responses in ECL, different paths and optional decisions are presented, which, when tested, show relative problem solving and critical thinking skills.

6. **Level of utilization-**

    Good training must result in changed behavior in the workplace. It isn't only what learner's know or how they solve problems. It's also what they DO with that knowledge, and how much better they perform, i.e. efficiency, less down time, increased productivity, etc.

    Utilization is not easy to measure, but with ECL and e-learning, these outcomes are more easily calibrated. Emotion is the key dynamic that allows this to happen. ECL provides tools to enable "real-time" monitoring of on-the-job-performance.

7. **Transfer-**

    Using motivation, incentives and reinforcements that tie directly to the learning experience, tangible and nearly immediate returns are identifiable usually within 30 to 120 days. This means the creation of value and true "business results."

8. **ROI-**

    Impact upon the bottom line; reducing costs, increased levels of productivity and revenue enhancements. (See case studies on preceding pages). There are other elements of a "business result" approach as well that consistently appeal to businessmen including: shifting fixed costs to variable ones, unit cost reductions, buying in volume, system and process efficiency that are also met through E-motionally Charged Learning.

9. **New knowledge-**

    Factual knowledge is relatively easy to measure. It is just as important, though, that the material is directed at specific learning objectives, which are tied to actual behavior in the workplace. The word we have used for this learning is "transfer."

Those are the overall, basic evaluations necessary and symbiotic to a full understanding of the benefits, costs and value of ECL and e-learning. The next technique of the three is: the financial model.

Financial model-
This technique must also be used with an eye toward a larger context of educational effectiveness. I don't need to tell you that e-learning costs and benefits need to produce tangible and clear financial rewards. Every other department within your company is subjected to this scrutiny, so e-learning and ECL must be graded on the same criteria.

In this regard, your organization must choose the definitions. Is cash flow more important than other financial considerations? How many years are needed to depreciate capital goods? How does your company define internal rates of return? Only you and your organization can examine your training investment against those kinds of criteria.

Finally, there is the Creation of Value model, or the ways that an organization improves, innovates and "competes." This technique is new, different and evolving. Considering that the most successful CEOs in the knowledge-based economy match these yardsticks, this is an important ingredient in the mix.

Creation of Value model-
Traditional ROI analyses are best suited to stable, consistent and predictable times and conditions. When is the next time you think you will see these criteria come together in your business?

The Internet has changed EVERYTHING! Time and knowledge are more important than ROI. Dramatic growth from new markets and INNOVATION are more important than the sometimes fictional bottom line. Obviously the term "value" will mean different things to different people. With this in mind, I will try to abbreviate some of the issues that might be included in most CEO's list of values received from e-learning and ECL, not all of which directly relate to ROI.

In terms of business strategies the creation of value would have to include: improved shareholder returns, sales and revenue growth, a competitive advantage, expanding market share and reaching new ones.

Some considerations that may be more difficult to measure, but certainly no less important would be: the development of talent, the retention of that talent, an increased ability to innovate through the use of this talent, customer satisfaction, retention of customers, loyalty of customers, time to market and the time it takes to become competent.

PART FOUR

HOW CAN YOUR ORGANIZATION BENEFIT FROM EMOTIONALLY CHARGED LEARNING?

Throughout this book I have attempted to "build my case" for . . .

Emotionally Charged Learning . . .

. . . and in so doing have given you . . .

Secrets To Competitive Advantages In The Second Half of The Knowledge/Entertainment-Based Economy

We also discussed today's knowledge-based economy and I hope I gave you great reasons to pause and think about what is going on the world economy today, and the challenges we all face in not only keeping up, but leaping—no SOARING ahead of the competition. You have discovered the role that emotions play in learning in general. I've also discussed how emotions affect memory and the role that memory plays in learning in general.

In addition, we looked at mythology, its history and the importance of storytelling to the individual and to society, even in today's electronically driven world with computers, digital, video and voice recording technology to aid in the retention of knowledge.

I continued to build my case by looking at the importance of the history and modern day use of marketing and cinematic techniques, both of which are used to influence, persuade and teach, all through emotions and which are used to influence, persuade and teach, all through emotions and memory—all ECL techniques.

We talked about how important it is to insure that the knowledge that has been gained is then retained and USED . . . efficiently and immediately. I even made a strong case for return on your investment in Emotionally Charged Learning and showed you the obvious and not so obvious ways that it is all very profitable.

In addition to these important issues, I also hope I conveyed what I feel are the responsibilities we have to help people become the best they can be, and in turn, hope they do the same for society.

I believe passionately that ECL is the content and vehicle for the mythology of the 21st century. And I believe in my heart that Emotionally Charged Learning is the absolute best way to keep bettering society by enhancing the awareness, skills, competency and productivity of our people.

I've said this before but it is important to repeat: Emotionally Charged Learning is truly a modern day extension of what our ancestors used to be—storytellers, facilitators of knowledge, and creators of mythology. Before the written word, storytellers transferred information and knowledge to their own communities and beyond as well as to younger generations for three reasons:

- To teach people how to survive
- To teach people how to better themselves and society
- To entertain them . . .

ECL does the same thing using the same techniques:

- Emotion
- Memory
- Fun

After all, we have no choice. We don't sit by the fire sharing our stories anymore (unless we're camping). Unfortunately we don't even sit around the dinner table as a family every night and share stories as much as we once did. (Personally, I find that very sad, not to mention it is a loss of a great source of knowledge and understanding).

Because we live in a hyper-paced, omni-technological, global, knowledge and entertainment-based economy, it has become necessary to tell our stories differently, using the most efficient tools available. Once that was cuneiform on clay tablets; then it was through the printing press; then along came the telephone, television, movies and now, finally the computer and the Internet.

For these reasons the teaching we do, the storytelling, must be HIGHLY SOPHISTICATED EMOTIONALLY CHARGED ENTERTAINMENT. We must compete for people's ATTENTION in a way the world has never been faced with. (If you're a parent you know just how difficult it is to get and maintain your child's attention in today's world, not to mention teaching him or her something of lasting value).

Not only must we compete to get their attention, and then give them "off-the-charts" training, we must provide them with stimulating, compelling, engaging, mind-blowing content that is retained and then immediately utilized (transferred to the workplace in tangible, meaningful, high-return-on-investment ways!).

You are now aware of the current realities in our knowledge/entertainment-based economy and you fully understand the importance of Emotionally Charged Learning. Now it is time to harness this information and use it to ride the crest of the wave that is the second half of this economy. Remember, technology is not compassionate, sympathetic or gentle, and by extension, neither is our economy. Technology crashes into existing systems with a take-no-prisoners approach while it simultaneously destroys them, creating new ones in its wake.

Your only true defense is knowledge, your people, your human capital. How will you put that capital to work?

The world is charged with emotion as well as intellect. We are living in the most competitive environment humankind has ever known, a highly sophisticated economy that literally changes day by day.

How will you and your company approach it? How will you not only keep up, but exceed beyond your current dreams? I wish you all the success in the world.

Eric Schiffer